PHILIPPIANS & COLOSSIANS

Also by Tara-Leigh Cobble

The Bible Recap:
A One-Year Guide to Reading and Understanding the Entire Bible
The Bible Recap Study Guide:
Daily Questions to Deepen Your Understanding of the Entire Bible
The Bible Recap Journal:
Your Daily Companion to the Entire Bible
The Bible Recap Discussion Guide:
Weekly Questions for Group Conversation on the Entire Bible
The Bible Recap Kids' Devotional:
365 Reflections and Activities for Children and Families
The God Shot:
100 Snapshots of God's Character in Scripture
Israel: *Beauty, Light, and Luxury*
The Bible Recap for Kids:
A 365-Day Guide Through the Bible for Young Readers
The Bible Recap 365-Day Chronological Study Bible:
English Standard Version

THE BIBLE RECAP KNOWING JESUS SERIES*

Knowing Jesus as King: *A 10-Session Study on the Gospel of Matthew*
Knowing Jesus as Servant: *A 10-Session Study on the Gospel of Mark*
Knowing Jesus as Savior: *A 10-Session Study on the Gospel of Luke*
Knowing Jesus as God: *A 10-Session Study on the Gospel of John*

THE BIBLE RECAP KNOWING GOD SERIES*

Acts: *The Spirit and the Bride—*
a 10-Week Bible Study on God and His Church
Romans: *Dead to Sin and Alive to Christ—*
a 10-Week Bible Study
1 & 2 Corinthians: *Love, Unity, and the Countercultural*
Power of the Cross—a 10-Week Bible Study
Galatians & Ephesians: *The Freedom and Purpose in*
the Body of Christ—a 10-Week Bible Study

* General editor

THE BIBLE RECAP KNOWING GOD SERIES

PHILIPPIANS & COLOSSIANS

HUMILITY, LOVE, AND TRUTH

A 10-WEEK BIBLE STUDY
ON THE DEITY OF CHRIST

TARA-LEIGH COBBLE,
GENERAL EDITOR

WRITTEN BY THE D-GROUP THEOLOGY & CURRICULUM TEAM

BETHANYHOUSE
a division of Baker Publishing Group
Minneapolis, Minnesota

Published by Bethany House Publishers
Minneapolis, Minnesota
BethanyHouse.com

Bethany House Publishers is a division of
Baker Publishing Group, Grand Rapids, Michigan

Printed in the United States of America

Library of Congress Cataloging-in-Publication Data
Names: Cobble, Tara-Leigh editor
Title: Philippians & Colossians : humility, love, and truth : a 10-week Bible study on the deity of Christ / Tara-Leigh Cobble.
Other titles: Philippians and Colossians
Description: Minneapolis, Minnesota : Bethany House Publishers, a division of Baker Publishing Group, [2025] | Series: The Bible recap knowing God series | Includes bibliographical references.
Identifiers: LCCN 2025037460 | ISBN 9780764245886 paperback | ISBN 9781493452453 ebook
Subjects: LCSH: Bible. Philippians—Study and teaching | Bible. Philippians—Commentaries | Bible. Colossians—Study and teaching | Bible. Colossians—Commentaries | Jesus Christ—Divinity—Biblical teaching
Classification: LCC BS2705.55 .P445 2025
LC record available at https://lccn.loc.gov/2025037460

The D-Group Theology & Curriculum Team is Laura Buchelt, Emily Pickell, Abbey Dane, Kirsten McCloskey, Emma Dotter, Liz Suggs, and Tara-Leigh Cobble.

The general editor is represented by Alive Literary Agency, AliveLiterary.com.

Cover design by Dan Pitts

Baker Publishing Group publications use paper produced from sustainable forestry practices and postconsumer waste whenever possible.

25 26 27 28 29 30 31 7 6 5 4 3 2 1

CONTENTS

HOW TO USE THIS STUDY

While Bible study is vital to the Christian walk, a well-rounded spiritual life comes from engaging with other spiritual disciplines as well. This study is designed not only to equip you with greater knowledge and theological depth, but to help you engage in other formative practices that will create a fuller, more fulfilling relationship with Jesus. We want to see you thrive in every area of your life with God!

Content and Questions

In each of the ten weeks of this study, the teaching and questions are divided into six days, but feel free to do it all at once if that's more manageable for your schedule. If you choose to complete each week's study in one sitting (especially if that time occurs later in the study-week), keep in mind that there are aspects you will want to be mindful of each day: the daily Bible reading, Scripture memorization, and the weekly challenge. Those are best attended to throughout the week.

Daily Bible Reading

The daily Bible reading corresponds to our study. It will take an average of three minutes per day to simply read (not study) the text. If you're an auditory learner, you may prefer to listen to an audio version of these Bible chapters.

Even if you decide to do the week's content and questions in one sitting, we still encourage you to make the daily Bible reading a part of your regular daily rhythm. Establishing a habit of reading the Word every day will help fortify your faith and create greater connection with God.

If you decide to break the study up into the six allotted days each week, your daily Bible reading will align with your study. Days 1–5 will follow our study of Philippians and Colossians, Day 6 features a psalm that corresponds to our reading, and Day 7 serves as a catch-up day in case you fall behind.

Scripture Memorization

Memorizing Scripture isn't busywork! It's an important part of hiding God's Word in our hearts (Psalm 119:11). Our first memorization passage—Philippians 2:5–11—focuses on the humility and love Jesus demonstrated when He came to earth to be our Savior. And our second memorization passage—Colossians 1:15–20—centers on the deity of Jesus Christ, who was fully God and fully man. We encourage you to practice the verses cumulatively—that is, *add* to what you're practicing each week instead of *replacing* it. We quote the English Standard Version (and some of our resources are in that translation as well), but feel free to memorize them in whatever translation you prefer. We suggest working on each week's verse(s) throughout the week, not just at the last minute. We've provided some free tools to help you with this, including a weekly verse song: MyDGroup.org/Resources/PhilCol.

Weekly Challenge

This is our practical response to what we've learned each week. We want to be "doers of the word, and not hearers only" (James 1:22). You'll find a variety of challenges, and we encourage you to lean into them all—especially the ones you find *most* challenging! This will help strengthen your spiritual muscles and encourage you in your faith. As with the memory verse, you'll want to begin this practice earlier in the week, especially because some weekly challenges include things to do each day of the week (e.g., prayers, journaling, etc.).

Resources

This is a Scripture-heavy study, and you'll find yourself looking up passages often. If you're new to studying Scripture, this will be a great way to dig in and sharpen your skills! You will feel more equipped and less intimidated as you move through each chapter. Some questions may ask you to refer to a Bible dictionary, commentary, or Greek or Hebrew lexicon, but you don't need to purchase those tools. There are lots of free options available online. We've linked to some of our favorite tools—plus additional resources such as podcasts, articles, and apps—at MyDGroup.org/Resources/PhilCol.

Groups

Because each week has a lot of questions in the content, we offer the following recommendation for those who plan to discuss the study in a weekly group meeting. As each member is doing their homework, we suggest they mark their favorite items with a star and mark any confusing items with a question mark. This serves as preparation for the group discussion and helps direct the conversation in beneficial ways. Group leaders, please note the starred prompt(s) in each chapter; we've highlighted these for you as topics you may find helpful to prioritize in group discussions.

INTRODUCTION TO PHILIPPIANS

On Paul's second missionary journey, he stopped in Philippi (Acts 12), a prominent Roman city in the Macedonian province. While observing the Sabbath with a group of women by a river outside of town, Paul met and ministered to a woman named Lydia. She and her entire household believed the gospel, and the Philippian church was born.

This fledgling church also came to include the entire household of the jailer whose life was spared when Paul and Silas opted not to leave their miraculously opened prison cells. The men and women of the Philippian church were dear to Paul, and they faithfully supported his ministry—both financially and relationally—from the start. As you study this letter, you'll see evidence of their close friendship.

Most scholars believe Paul wrote this letter to the Philippian church while he was imprisoned in Rome between AD 60 and 62. This Roman imprisonment was likely different from how we think of incarceration today. While we don't know for certain whether Paul was under house arrest or in a physical jail cell in chains, he likely had to provide for himself to meet his basic needs. But he could receive visitors—including various ministry partners—and he wrote several of his New Testament letters during this time.

Though Paul's letter to the Philippians is more personal and practical than theological, he still includes rich and profound teachings about Jesus. Paul's tone is one of encouragement and love rather than warnings and correction (like we see in many of his other letters). The major themes include pursuing Christlikeness, the importance of prayer, unity, and—most importantly—joy. Paul mentions joy or rejoicing sixteen times throughout the letter, which is especially noteworthy given that he was writing from captivity.

Why would he write a letter to his friends about joy while imprisoned in Rome? Let's find out together!

WEEK 1

Philippians 1:1–18

Scripture to Memorize

Have this mind among yourselves, which is yours in Christ Jesus . . .

Philippians 2:5

Note: If you haven't yet read How to Use This Study on page 7, please do that before continuing. It will provide you with a proper framework and helpful tools.

DAILY BIBLE READING

Day 1: Philippians 1:1–2
Day 2: Philippians 1:3–6
Day 3: Philippians 1:7–11
Day 4: Philippians 1:12–14
Day 5: Philippians 1:15–18
Day 6: Psalm 16
Day 7: Catch-Up Day

Corresponds to Day 351 of *The Bible Recap*.

WEEKLY CHALLENGE

See page 31 for more information.

DAY 1

Philippians 1:1–2

READ PHILIPPIANS 1:1–2

Review 1:1.

Like a well-trained teacher, Paul began his letter to the Philippians by modeling one of the key points of the letter: humility. He could have called attention to his distinct role as an apostle or to his Jewish heritage (e.g., Ephesians 1:1; 2 Corinthians 1:1), but he didn't. Right out of the gate, Paul the mentor put Timothy, his mentee, on his level, referring to them both as servants of Christ.

1. **Look up the word for *servants* (1:1) in a Greek lexicon and write what you find below.**

★ 2. If you were writing to believers at another church, how would you want to describe yourself?

★ 3. Would that description be accurate? Explain.

If someone wanted to know what the church in Philippi was like, a quick glance at 1:1 would help. The two servants (Paul and Timothy) wrote to three distinct groups of people: saints, overseers, and deacons. The presence of these three groups indicated that the church was well established and organized—from the general to the specific.

In Philippi, the church leadership structure likely looked like this:[1]

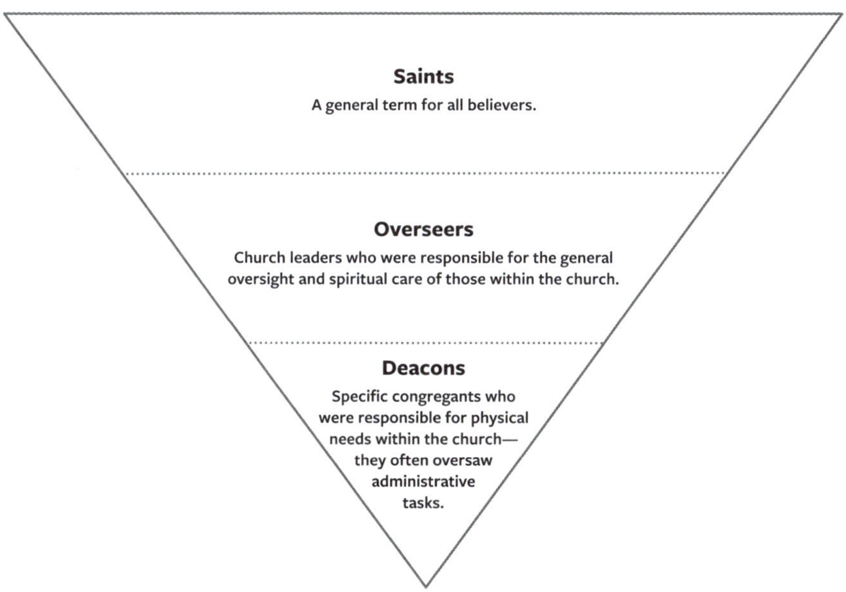

4. Based on the text and the chart above, who is a saint?

A. A specific believer who was exceptionally faithful and is now deceased
B. A player on a professional sports team
C. Anyone who is a Christian
D. Someone who goes above and beyond in their charity work or has a unique anointing in certain spiritual gifts or in performing miracles

Review 1:2.

5. Using a Bible dictionary, match each term with its definition.

Grace	The gift of God's generosity, kindness, and favor toward those who don't deserve it
Peace	The gift of a quieted and calmed spirit, regardless of one's circumstances, that can come only from God

Once again, Paul and Timothy modeled what they'd later teach. Their greeting was a demonstration of unity, as they paired the traditional Greek greeting—grace (*charis*)—with the traditional Hebrew greeting—peace.

6. How many times did Paul mention Jesus as Christ in 1:1–2?

Believers—no matter their backgrounds—are unified *in* and *through* Christ. And in Paul's letter to this church, he leads with an emphasis on this otherwise-unattainable unity.

DAY 2

Philippians 1:3–6

READ PHILIPPIANS 1:3–6

Review 1:3–4.

Whenever Paul thought of the Philippians, he thanked God for them. His gratitude likely stemmed from their financial support and spiritual partnership. They were reliable teammates (4:14). But Paul didn't just *say* he prayed; he clarified *how* he prayed.

1. How did Paul "make" his prayer?

Biblical joy doesn't refer solely to traditional happiness or glee; it can accompany experiences that look more like valleys than mountaintops. It's rooted in a pervasive confidence in God's sovereignty and character. The heart marked by joy ultimately says, *"No matter what happens, God is still good. I can trust Him. He's worthy of my praise. I will praise Him in this moment, and in the next, with gladness in my heart."*

This confidence leads believers to enjoy Jesus more fully, because *He's where the joy is*—no matter our circumstances. A byproduct of biblical joy is contentment. When biblical joy is present, our circumstances might not change, but our perspective will.

2. Throughout Philippians, Paul modeled principles of biblical joy. Based on context clues in the descriptions below, match each attribute of biblical joy to its appropriate description.

Biblical joy is:

Inclusive	It's expressed through love for (and partnership with) other believers (1:4).
Gospel-Fueled	Biblical joy can exist in the toughest of circumstances (4:11–13).
Christ-Centered	Christians who are marked by joy aren't focused on themselves or their circumstances. They're focused on Christ (2:2).
Suffering-Resistant	Biblical joy is a byproduct of the gospel being proclaimed to those who haven't heard it (1:18).

Paul's prayers were also marked by gratitude. This gratitude was both horizontal—Paul was grateful for the faithful saints in Philippi—and vertical—Paul recognized that what he saw in the Philippians was a result of *God's* work in their lives.

3. When Paul thought about the Philippians, his prayers were marked by gratitude and joy. Write a joyful prayer expressing gratitude for a believer who has made an impact on your life.

Review 1:5.

4. Fill in the blank on the timeline below. Then across the timeline's gap, explain why Paul said he thanked God for the Philippians.

The First Day ____________

Review 1:6.

5. The NASB reads, "For I am *confident* of this very thing" (emphasis added). **Using a thesaurus, list a few synonyms for *confident*.**

★ 6. Extend the timeline in today's fourth prompt. What was Paul confident would happen? And when?

What God initiates He will sustain and He will fulfill. It's like Paul was saying, *"I've cheered you on, I'm cheering for you now, and I'm going to continue cheering for you, because I know our God is going to finish what He started."* Paul was confident the Philippians would be fully conformed to the image of Christ, and we can be confident the same is true for us!

DAY 3

Philippians 1:7–11

READ PHILIPPIANS 1:7–11

★ 1. Why was Paul imprisoned? What might prison have been like? (Hint: Review the introduction on page 11 for help.)

Review 1:7–8.

Paul's affection for the Philippians was tried and true!

2. Fill in the blanks in 1:7 below.

"You are all partakers with me of ________________________, both in my ________________________, and in the ________________________, and ________________________ of the ________________________."

Calling to mind legal proceedings, Paul referenced a well-structured argument or "verbal defense."[1] Paul and the Philippians were prepared to defend their beliefs, but the gospel was confirmed (validated) in front of others whenever people accepted its message and were transformed.

Because it is the foundation of our faith and Paul's message, it's important that we clarify what the gospel is and isn't.

The gospel is the good news of how faith in Jesus's life, death, burial, and resurrection saves people from sin and brings them to God (Colossians 1:13). Sin is anything that misses the mark—falling short of God's standard of perfection—and all people are sinners (Romans 3:23). Sin earns us death and eternal separation from God (Romans 5:8). Nothing we can do (or the Philippians could've done) can save us from sin. Even our best "good works" fall short of God's standard (Titus 3:5).

But God the Father sent Jesus to take the punishment we deserve for our sin (John 3:16). Jesus died on the cross and rose from the grave three days later, defeating sin and death forever! When people become "partakers of grace" and place their faith in Jesus, like Paul and the Philippians did, they've received the *free gift* of salvation (Ephesians 2:8–9) and the deposit of the Holy Spirit (2 Corinthians 1:22), and they live differently because of it (Romans 10:9–10). Humans can't earn salvation, but a holy God offers it freely—and *that's* the beauty of the gospel.

3. Paul was both brilliant and deeply relational. His letter to the Philippians was more personal than his other letters. How did he express his affection for them? Where did that affection come from?

Review 1:9–11.

Even though the Philippians were already saints, Paul prayed they'd grow. The power and truth of the gospel isn't something Christians outgrow—we need reminders and encouragement. Becoming a Christian doesn't mean we no longer sin—it means those sins are *paid for*, and it means we have the Holy Spirit to help us overcome temptation and grow in Christlikeness.

4. In 1:9–10, what three things did Paul pray for? Why did Paul want the Philippians to have them?

Being "pure and blameless" doesn't mean being perfect, at least not while we're on this broken planet. Purity is living a life marked by integrity—no secrets. Blamelessness is maintaining a strong, godly reputation. Not only is God glorified in this, but it sets Christians apart in the eyes of the world.

★ 5. Where does the "fruit of righteousness" come from?

When people become Christians, they're sealed with the Holy Spirit (Ephesians 1:13–14). Jesus sent the Spirit, and He called the Spirit the "Helper" (John 14:16). The Spirit empowers Christians to live differently. The Philippians weren't immediately pure and blameless, but as they'd respond to the Spirit, they'd start to look more and more like Jesus—and when they'd finally see Jesus face-to-face, they'd look just like Him!

6. Describe a time when you tried to change on your own. How might it have been different if you had depended on the Holy Spirit?

DAY 4

Philippians 1:12–14

READ PHILIPPIANS 1:12–14

Review 1:12.

1. What phrase indicates that Paul was revealing the reason he wrote this letter?

Up to this point in the letter Paul had been "warming up." He'd provided a framework for his relationship with the Philippians and called attention to the gospel power that was already at work in them. Here, he began to explain his motives: He wanted to expand the Philippians' understanding of difficult circumstances.

2. **Look back at the introduction (page 11) or use a Bible study tool, then fill in the flowchart below.**

What happened to Paul?	→	What was the result (1:12)?

Review 1:13.

Paul's continued faithfulness, despite his undesirable circumstances, opened the door for truth to reach even more people. *God was at work!* From prison, Paul was able to share the gospel with people he would have never had access to otherwise: elite soldiers of the Roman military, the "imperial guard."

Additionally, Paul shared that his imprisonment had been a testimony to "the rest." This likely meant that no one thought Paul was in prison because he'd committed a ghastly crime, like stealing or murder. Everyone knew he was in prison for preaching the gospel. So the message of the gospel continued to extend far beyond his chains whenever people talked or thought about him.

Review 1:14.

So how did other believers respond to Paul's situation? His brothers in Christ were inspired—they were moved to more boldly proclaim the gospel in response to what they saw God doing through him.

Remember, Paul's boldness was what led to his arrest; but paradoxically, his arrest led to the gospel spreading with even more boldness. His arrest fueled the emboldening of others, putting them at a greater risk of being arrested too. What could have sparked fear inspired courage and zeal.

Adversity can be a surprisingly effective platform for the spreading of the gospel. Paul and "the brothers" understood that when the rubber meets the road, or when life is just more challenging than usual, the opportunities for the gospel to spread are endless.

★ 3. Are there any circumstances in your life that you need God to help you reframe as gospel opportunities? Journal a prayer asking God to embolden you.

★ 4. How specifically can you lean into these opportunities to share the gospel? List possible next steps below, then pray through them. Ask God to show you what's next.

DAY 5

Philippians 1:15–18

READ PHILIPPIANS 1:15–18

Review 1:15.

Some people were preaching Christ with impure motives. The Philippians were aware of this, so it seems Paul wanted them to understand how *he* thought about those people and their motives.

1. **Using a dictionary, match each term with its corresponding definition.**

Envy	Feeling a strong sense of competition
Rivalry	Feeling discontent or covetousness in response to what someone else has

You may be wondering, *Why would anyone envy Paul if preaching the gospel led to his imprisonment?*

Review 1:16–18.

Paul made it clear that those who preached the gospel out of love were motivated by their love for Christ, and they recognized that they were on the same team as Paul. They were all on mission *together*. On the contrary, those who preached from a place of envy or rivalry may have been jealous of Paul's influence. Perhaps they wanted a larger personal platform (more followers), or perhaps some minor doctrinal disagreements fueled competitive spirits.

One thing was clear: These people were preaching *the actual gospel* (which we studied in depth on Day 3). Elsewhere, Paul addressed those who were preaching a *false* gospel. He had incredibly harsh words for them: "Let him be accursed" (see Galatians 1:6–10). But that isn't the case here. These people were preaching the Truth (John 14:6), and *the Truth* is what makes the difference in Paul's responses.

2. According to 1:17, why did some people preach from selfish ambition?

The Greek word for *selfish ambition* (*eritheia*), was used to describe "the ruthlessly ambitious—those who sought to elevate themselves at all costs."[1] These preachers were intentionally undermining Paul. Because Paul was giving his life for the sake of the gospel, this could have caused him some brief sadness at minimum. But it also had the potential to deeply discourage or depress him throughout his imprisonment. If you were one of the Philippians and you knew a group of people were opposing your friend Paul, wouldn't you want to respond to them—and perhaps defensively?

3. What was Paul's response?

Paul was confident that God is the one who deals with the motives of the messengers. That wasn't Paul's responsibility nor was it the Philippians'.

It's been said that it's important to "keep the main thing the main thing."[2] And that's exactly what Paul did. He was glad the truth of Jesus was being proclaimed—regardless of the messenger's motive. So Paul rejoiced in Christ. Despite Paul's challenging circumstances, he always remembered and reminded others of the confidence we can find only in Jesus. He's where the joy is!

★ 4. What stood out to you most in this week's study? Why?

★ 5. What did you learn or relearn about God and His character this week?

DAY 6

Corresponding Psalm & Prayer

READ PSALM 16

1. What correlation do you see between Psalm 16 and this week's study?

2. What portions of this psalm stand out to you most?

3. Close by praying this prayer aloud:

Father,

My heart is glad and my whole being rejoices! The boundary lines have fallen for me in pleasant places. Indeed, I have a beautiful inheritance—now and forever! In Your presence, there is fullness of joy.

God, You have saved me, but I'm still a sinner. I'm Your servant, but sometimes I still act like You owe me something for following You. I am unified with my brothers and sisters in and through Your Son, but sometimes I sow division with my bickering and petty disagreement. I balk at hardship of any kind, but Your Spirit empowers me to endure so much more for the sake of the gospel. I repent of all this and more. I have no good apart from You.

Make known to me the path of life. Help me to keep the main thing the main thing—and that's you, Lord! Help me to believe down to my bones that no matter what happens, You are still good. I can trust You. You are worthy of my praise. I will praise You in this moment, and in the next, with gladness in my heart.

I surrender my life to You, Lord—every moment of my day, each decision I make, I yield my will and way to Your perfect will and way.

I love You too. Amen.

DAY 7

Rest, Catch Up, or Dig Deeper

WEEKLY CHALLENGE

On Day 2, you filled in a timeline that portrayed Paul's relationship with the Philippians and his prayer for their continued growth. This week, create your own spiritual timeline. On the left side, write "birth," and on the other end write "the day of Christ Jesus." Along the timeline, plot three to five things that have significantly impacted you and/or your spiritual growth. What have you seen God do throughout your life? Use whatever creative tools you have on hand to document your life. You can even add photos if you'd like!

WEEK 2

Philippians 1:19–30

Scripture to Memorize

. . . who, though he was in the form of God, did not count equality with God a thing to be grasped, but emptied himself, by taking the form of a servant, being born in the likeness of men.

Philippians 2:6–7

DAILY BIBLE READING

Day 1: Philippians 1:19–20
Day 2: Philippians 1:21–23
Day 3: Philippians 1:24–26
Day 4: Philippians 1:27–28
Day 5: Philippians 1:29–30
Day 6: Psalm 3
Day 7: Catch-Up Day

Corresponds to Day 351 of *The Bible Recap.*

WEEKLY CHALLENGE

See page 51 for more information.

DAY 1

Philippians 1:19–20

READ PHILIPPIANS 1:19–20

Bible translators added chapter and verse numbers many years after Paul wrote this letter to the Philippians. So if it seems like he was in the middle of a thought here, it's because he was. Let's go back to review his train of thought.

1. According to 1:18, what did Paul rejoice in?

Review 1:18b–19.

Paul's situation wasn't looking good. Having been mocked (Acts 17:32), beaten (Acts 16:19–24), and handed over to Roman authorities by his fellow Jewish leaders (Acts 21:26–27), he was in captivity, awaiting trial (Acts 28:16–31). But against all odds, he was *rejoicing*. How was that even possible? Paul credited two factors.

2. Use 1:19 to fill in the blanks below.

"For I know that ______________ ______________ ______________ and the help of the ______________ ______________ ______________ ______________ this will turn out for my deliverance."

The power of the Spirit is unparalleled, and the power of prayer is indisputable. Knowing that these saints were already praying for him, Paul was basically telling them, "*Your prayers for me have given me a constant awareness of the Spirit's presence and help in the midst of my trials.*"

So, bolstered by the prayers of this church that was incredibly dear to him, Paul rejoiced, sure that deliverance was coming. Paul didn't explicitly tell the Philippians what his deliverance would look like, and we don't have any evidence from the text that Paul knew exactly what God had planned for him either. His deliverance could have been immediate or eternal.

★ 3. Complete the table below.

Paul's Hardships

What would immediate deliverance have looked like?	What would eternal deliverance have looked like?

While both types of deliverance certainly would have brought relief, there's a clue in the original language that points us to the source of Paul's joyful confidence.

★ 4. **Use a Greek lexicon to look up the word that many of our English Bibles translate as *deliverance* (1:19).** What is the word in Greek? What is its literal meaning?

★ 5. What does that tell you about where Paul's confidence came from?

Review 1:20.

A right understanding and holy fear of our righteous, eternal God puts everything else into perspective. Paul knew that his trials—though they were many—were temporary; death would end them. Paul also knew that as long as he had life and breath in his body, he would honor Christ. For him, shame didn't come from mockery or abuse or arrest or captivity. In other words, absolutely nothing anyone could do to him could bring Paul shame. Shame could only come from dishonoring Christ. But in *honoring* Christ? Whether living or dying, Paul would "not be at all ashamed."

DAY 2

Philippians 1:21–23

READ PHILIPPIANS 1:21–23

Whether Paul lived or died, his singular focus was Christ. Living meant more time to know Christ and to make Christ known. And dying?

Review 1:21.

1. How did Paul describe death?

As the *Enduring Word* commentary puts it, "Paul knew that death was not a defeat to the Christian. It is merely a graduation to glory, a net gain."[1]

Review 1:22.

As a Roman citizen, Paul considered taking his case directly to the Roman emperor (Acts 25:11; 28:19). But even in exercising his civil right to the appeal process, his purpose in living was "fruitful labor": to do earthly work that would have eternal impact.

★ 2. What kind of "fruitful labor" had Paul already done for Christ and His church? Use a Bible study tool or do a web search for help if needed.

If his appeal to the Roman emperor led to his release, Paul would have more work to do. But if his case wasn't decided in his favor, Paul was ready to die. He summed up his options like this: "I really don't know which is better" (NLT).

For believers whose entire hope is securely in Jesus, life—even life marked by hardship and suffering—is an opportunity for fruitful labor. And death isn't just an end to suffering; it's the beginning of an eternity in Jesus's presence.

Core beliefs of the Christian faith have been outlined in a series of questions and answers called a catechism. In 1563, the writers of the Heidelberg Catechism put it this way:

> Question: What is your only comfort in life and death?
>
> Answer: That I am not my own, but belong with body and soul, both in life and in death, to my faithful Savior Jesus Christ.[2]

★ 3. In your own words, how would you answer this question asked in the Heidelberg Catechism? What is your only comfort in life and death?

Review 1:23.

Death itself isn't desirable; it's an inevitable, heartbreaking consequence of living in our fallen world. But death in Christ is something altogether different. Paul desired death, not because he wanted an escape from his trials, but because he longed for eternity in the presence of his faithful Savior.

For the believer facing trials, we don't need to look to death as a means of escape from our present reality. No matter what we're up against, the Spirit of God dwells in us and empowers us for every second we live, whether it's joyful or excruciating. But we can—and should—look to death as the beginning of our eternal reward. And with that posture, we join our brother Paul in declaring, "When God calls me, I can't wait to go home."

DAY 3

Philippians 1:24–26

READ PHILIPPIANS 1:24–26

Having just written this about living and dying: "I really don't know which is better" (1:22 NLT), it seems that Paul had made up his mind.

Review 1:24.

★ 1. What was "more necessary," according to Paul? Does this strike you as a change from 1:22–23? Why or why not?

Review 1:25.

There's still no evidence in the text that would lead us to believe God had given Paul specific insight into his future. But we have heaps of textual evidence that proves Paul had a godly understanding of his present.

2. Use each listed reference to complete the table below.

1:1	How did Paul describe himself?	
1:22	How did Paul describe his work?	

Paul wrote—and lived—with openhanded conviction. He was certain of his eternal home, yet confident in his present calling. He was convinced there was still work to be done, and as long as he was still breathing—no matter who tried to stop him and no matter what happened to him—he would do what God had called him to do.

3. What was Paul's purpose in remaining with the church?

Review 1:26.

4. Circle the underlined words or phrases that best complete each sentence below. Read 1:26 in a few different translations (NIV, NLT, CSB, etc.) for extra support if needed.

Paul wanted to visit the Philippians / go to trial, which would bring the Philippians anxiety / joy.

The Philippians would boast in Jesus / Paul because of all the cool things Paul would do / all the ways He would work through Paul.

Paul was convinced that he'd live a while longer because God had more work for him to do. But don't mistake his confidence for arrogance. Paul's conviction wasn't about himself at all; it was about Jesus and His church. Because Jesus "loved the church and gave himself up for her" (Ephesians

5:25), Paul was committed to the church's growth, encouragement, and instruction. And he knew that as the church grew to become more like Jesus, the believers' joy would grow too.

★ 5. How does growth in Christ lead to more joy?

DAY 4

Philippians 1:27–28

READ PHILIPPIANS 1:27–28

Paul was a man on a mission, but *not* a solo mission. He knew that his brothers and sisters—including his dear friends the Philippians—joined him in fruitful labor. So he encouraged them in their godly conduct.

Review 1:27a.

Your Bible may include a footnote that explains the sentiment of the original Greek word Paul used: *politeuomai*. Throughout his letters, Paul instructed many churches on how to conduct themselves as followers of Christ. But when writing to the Philippians, Paul used this particular word—one he didn't use in any of his other letters.

1. **Use a Greek lexicon to look up *politeuomai*** (1:27). What does it mean?

Philippi was a Roman city, and in the first century, Roman citizenship was a big deal. Roman citizens had privileges like property ownership, voting rights, and military protection. In return, their utmost loyalty was expected; above all else was their *civitas*—their Roman citizenship.[1]

But a Christian's ultimate loyalty isn't to their earthly nation; it's to their eternal King. Believers are citizens of Christ's everlasting kingdom.

And with a single word, Paul affirmed and aligned the right place for the Philippians'—and our—allegiance.

When Paul was writing this letter, the Roman Empire seemed indestructible. But like every empire before and after it, Rome eventually fell. Christ-followers are citizens in the only kingdom that will last forever. So Paul went on to describe how the Philippians should conduct themselves—not as citizens of an empire that would fall, but as citizens of a kingdom that will last forever.

Review 1:27b–28a.

2. What did Paul want to be *so true* about the Philippian church that he would hear about it from far away, even if he never got to see it in person? Complete the list below.

- Standing ________ in one ________
- Having one ________
- Striving ________ by ________ for the ________ of the ________
- ________ frightened in anything by your ________

Like a military leader inspiring his troops, Paul charged the Philippians to prepare for battle. And what were they fighting for? The gospel, of course—the good news that God sent His Son Jesus to pay the penalty for our sins, defeat death, and make a way for us to be with Him forever in His kingdom.

So to fight for the expansion of the gospel, Paul urged the Philippians—this citizen army—to stand firmly together, sure of their mission, unwavering in their conviction, and undeterred, even by their enemies.

★ 3. How would divisions among the Philippians have hindered their mission? How do divisions among believers today hinder our mission?

Review 1:28b.

Paul said the Philippians' unity would be a sign of destruction to their opponents. In most battles, there are signs of defeat, but not necessarily destruction. But the Philippians were preparing for a battle on behalf of a kingdom that will never end. Defeat would be too small. Enemies of the gospel who actively work against it won't just be defeated; they'll be destroyed. It's worth noting that one of the definitions of *destruction* here includes "eternal misery in hell."[2]

★ 4. According to 1:28, the Philippians' unity signaled their opponents' destruction. What else did it signal? How is that different from a victory?

DAY 5

Philippians 1:29–30

READ PHILIPPIANS 1:29–30

For modern audiences who live in places with religious freedom, the picture of the church as an army fighting battles for the gospel might seem a bit extreme. But to first-century churches across the region, the metaphor would have been comforting. Early Christ-followers were no strangers to violent persecution.

1. Why would each of the following groups have felt so threatened by Christianity that they resorted to violence against those who spread it? Use a Bible study tool or do a web search to help you if needed.

Roman government leaders:

Jewish religious leaders:

Review 1:29.

Without a doubt, believing in Jesus is a privilege—one that is granted to believers by God. Similarly, Paul taught that *suffering* for Jesus is also a privilege granted to believers by God. And this wasn't the first time that New Testament believers encountered this idea.

★ 2. Look up each of the passages below and complete the table.

Passage	What does it teach about persecution, tribulation, and suffering?
Matthew 5:10–12	
John 16:33	
Acts 5:41	

Everyday human experience tells us that without faith, suffering can be unbearable. But throughout the New Testament, we learn a new truth as believers: Suffering for Jesus's sake builds maturity (Romans 5:3–5). When believers suffer for the Lord, they grow in peace, understanding, trust, and joy.

So how is suffering a privilege? Because it can lead to a more mature faith, and it can provide opportunities for the gospel to spread. And Paul knew this from experience.

Review 1:30.

3. As a reminder, where was Paul writing from? Why was he there?

★ 4. What is the tone of Paul's letter?

A. Despair
B. Annoyance
C. Joy

It's worth reviewing: Given his present circumstances, how was that possible?

While the Roman government leaders hoped to subdue Paul (Acts 22; 24:27) and the Jewish religious leaders hoped to silence him (Acts 21–22), their plans didn't work. Suffering for Christ deepened Paul's faith. The more they fought him, the more he shared the gospel—urgently, boldly, and joyfully. Paul wanted everyone to know what he knew about Jesus: that beyond any doubt, He's where the joy is!

5. What stood out to you most in this week's study? Why?

6. What did you learn or relearn about God and His character this week?

DAY 6

Corresponding Psalm & Prayer

READ PSALM 3

1. What correlation do you see between Psalm 3 and this week's study?

2. What portions of this psalm stand out to you most?

3. Close by praying this prayer aloud:

Father,

You are on Your holy hill, yet when I call out to You, You answer me! You are a shield about me, my glory, and the lifter of my head.

God, like David wrote, I lay down and slept last night, and I woke again this morning because You sustained me. Jesus, like Paul wrote, I rejoice any time You are proclaimed. And Spirit, no matter what I go through, You are with me, guiding me and helping me.

Even though You are holy and eternal, I've made much of myself. Even though You are the only one I should fear, I've been scared of being mocked, persecuted, or even inconvenienced. Even though You've made me a citizen of Your eternal kingdom, I've put my hope in earthly things that will fade away. Forgive me, Lord.

Remind me that I am not my own, but belong with body and soul, both in life and in death, to my faithful Savior Jesus Christ. Make me not at all ashamed—of You, of Your Son, or of Your Spirit's work within me. Whether I live or die, let me honor You.

I surrender my life to You, Lord—every moment of my day, each decision I make, I yield my will and way to Your perfect will and way.

I love You too. Amen.

DAY 7

Rest, Catch Up, or Dig Deeper

WEEKLY CHALLENGE

On Day 1, you reflected on Paul's hardships and what deliverance could have looked like for him. Complete the same table below—this time for yourself. What hardships are you facing?

Your Current Hardships

What would immediate deliverance look like?	What would eternal deliverance look like?

Review 1:18b–20. In your journal or in the space below, write how Christ can be honored in your current hardships, regardless of whether your deliverance is immediate or eternal.

WEEK 3

Philippians 2

Scripture to Memorize

And being found in human
form, he humbled himself
by becoming obedient
to the point of death,
even death on a cross.

Philippians 2:8

DAILY BIBLE READING

Day 1: Philippians 2:1–11

Day 2: Philippians 2:12–13

Day 3: Philippians 2:14–18

Day 4: Philippians 2:19–24

Day 5: Philippians 2:25–30

Day 6: Psalm 8

Day 7: Catch-Up Day

Corresponds to Day 351 of *The Bible Recap.*

WEEKLY CHALLENGE

See page 71 for more information.

DAY 1

Philippians 2:1–11

READ PHILIPPIANS 2:1–11

Review 2:1–4.

At the end of last week's study (1:27–30), Paul encouraged the Philippians in their external conflicts—those outside the church. And here, he exhorted them *inside* the church.

The word *encouragement* here is translated from the ancient Greek word *paraklesis*, which means much more than our modern idea of reassurance. It implies help or strengthening. Similarly, the Latin word for *comfort* (*fortis*) means "brave." In this ancient use, there's an implication of love and encouragement that compels a person toward bravery and strength.

Paul was a master encourager, and he challenged any thought of encouragement as a soft or fluffy concept. To fly past 2:1 considering it a smattering of comfy words would be to miss Paul's point. He was basically saying, "*If you have these tremendous, divine gifts from God, then do me a favor and use them*" (see 2:1–2), and "*Here's how to do that*" (see 2:3).

Note that in 2:3–4, Paul was specifically commenting on *selfish* ambition or rivalry, serving one's own interests instead of considering others. Not all ambition is selfish ambition. What matters is the focus of our ambition: glorifying God.

Ancient Greek culture considered humility a fault, not a virtue. So Christ, and then His followers—like Paul—had to teach in such a way as to guide these early churches for whom *humility* was a dirty word. Paul wasn't telling the Philippians to think *badly* of themselves; he was telling them to think *rightly* of themselves, and 2:5–11 showed them how. As sons and daughters of the Most High God, we're invited to the abundance of becoming more like Him.

Review 2:5–8.

1. What does 2:5 say about the mind of Christ?

Believers don't have to muster up this "mind" in their own strength—they have it (1 Corinthians 2:16) but must choose to walk in it.

A good illustration to help us understand 2:6–8 is one of a king who put aside his riches to live as a poor person. In this illustration, the riches are still his, but he chose humility. Likewise, Jesus didn't cling to the privilege of His deity, but chose to take the form of a servant.

The ancient Greek word for *taking* here is *labōn*, which implies an *addition*, not an exchange. *This is important: He didn't shed His deity for His humanity.* Being fully God, He *took on* the form of a servant.

★ 2. How does Jesus's humility challenge or encourage you in your own circumstances? Briefly describe a situation where the role you played felt "below you"—and where having the mind of Christ might turn that indignation on its head.

During this time, crucifixion was such a shameful death that it wasn't allowed for Roman citizens—Philippians included. And because Jesus obediently accepted His role to empty Himself in this manner, God the Father's role was to exalt Him.

Review 2:9–11.

In saying every knee will bow and every tongue will acknowledge Jesus, it's important to note that Paul wasn't saying everyone would be saved. He was referencing Isaiah 45:23, in which God foretold that everyone would *acknowledge* Yahweh as Lord. Some Roman emperors during this period demanded to be called "Lord" as an acknowledgment that they were a deity. Claiming to be part god served as an endorsement of their role as emperor. But Paul essentially said of Jesus, *"His name is Yahweh."* And at that name, every person—every emperor, every opponent, every mocking tongue, every believer, and every denier of His deity—will acknowledge that He is Lord.

Paul wasn't just reminding the Philippians of theological truths. He was inviting them to live in response to these truths.

★ 3. What has changed in your life because you have the mind of Christ?

DAY 2

Philippians 2:12–13

READ PHILIPPIANS 2:12–13

Today's passage is an example of why reading Scripture in context is key. When Paul wrote Philippians, it was a letter. As we've previously discussed, translators hadn't yet added verse numbers to help readers in their study, so it's important to note that today's passage flowed together as one thought. If we were to read 2:12 without 2:13, we'd miss the message God inspired Paul to write.

Bear that in mind as you engage with what may feel like a weighty call in 2:12. In 2:13, we'll see who really does the heavy lifting.

Review 2:12.

Great job! That's how Paul began today's passage. He told the Philippians to keep doing what they've been doing even more in his absence.

1. What did Paul call the Philippians in 2:12?

2. Was Paul addressing believers or unbelievers in this verse?

3. Which of the below correctly completes 2:12? "Work ______ your own salvation."

A. for

B. out

C. to earn

This verse has often been misunderstood to mean that believers must work *for* their salvation. But throughout Scripture, God tells us it is by grace we have been saved, through faith; not by works (see Ephesians 2:8–9). Our salvation is based solely on Christ's finished work—His life, death, resurrection, and ascension.

So what was Paul saying here? He was compelling the Philippians to let the reality of their salvation be worked into the reality of their everyday lives—like working a flavor into a dough. Jesus came to bring eternal salvation; He also came that we might "have life and have it more abundantly" (John 10:10). Paul encouraged the Philippians not to forfeit the great invitation to live in the fullness of what Christ won for them!

So what's with the "fear and trembling"? Paul was doing something really clever here.

4. **Look up the meaning of the Greek words for *fear* (*phobos*) and *trembling* (*tromos*) in 2:12.** Write what you find.

The definition of *tromos* implies an awareness of one's inability to complete requirements. This understanding tees up the reader to better receive the beauty of 2:13.

Review 2:13.

If 2:12 felt like a weighty burden, 2:13 brings a sigh of divine relief. *He does the doing!* Paul told the Philippians God was the one doing good works *through* them—and even creating the desire in them to do those things!

★ 5. Does that feel like a relief to you—to know God works in you, both to will and to work? Can you recall a time when you noticed Him doing that in your own life? Explain.

Lest you think this verse implies a passive couch potato existence, Paul's very clear: That's not it either. We've got a divine, cosmic dance going on here. We are God's handiwork—created for good works, which God prepared in advance for us to do (see Ephesians 2:10). He does the doing—*in us and through us!*

DAY 3

Philippians 2:14–18

READ PHILIPPIANS 2:14–18

As you complete today's study, keep yesterday's lesson in mind: He who was highest willingly humbled Himself out of obedience—and God the Father exalted Him.

Review 2:14–15.

Grumbling and *disputing* bring to mind the Israelites' grumbling at God in the wilderness. God called them a "crooked and twisted generation" (Deuteronomy 32:5). Paul may have been telling the Philippians not to grumble about one another, but it's more likely he was referring to grumbling *against God about circumstances*.

★ 1. Does Paul's encouragement to do "all things" without grumbling seem unrealistic? What have you learned about Paul's life so far that challenges your own thoughts?

Here's the best part: Paul didn't tell the Philippians to shine. He told them not to grumble, and as a result, they *would* shine. There's an element of faith here. Paul was telling the Philippians to pit their temptation to grumble and complain against the truth of what God's Word says, to remember what He ultimately accomplishes through all our trials and circumstances.

2. On the first two stars below, write or paraphrase Genesis 15:5 and Daniel 12:3.

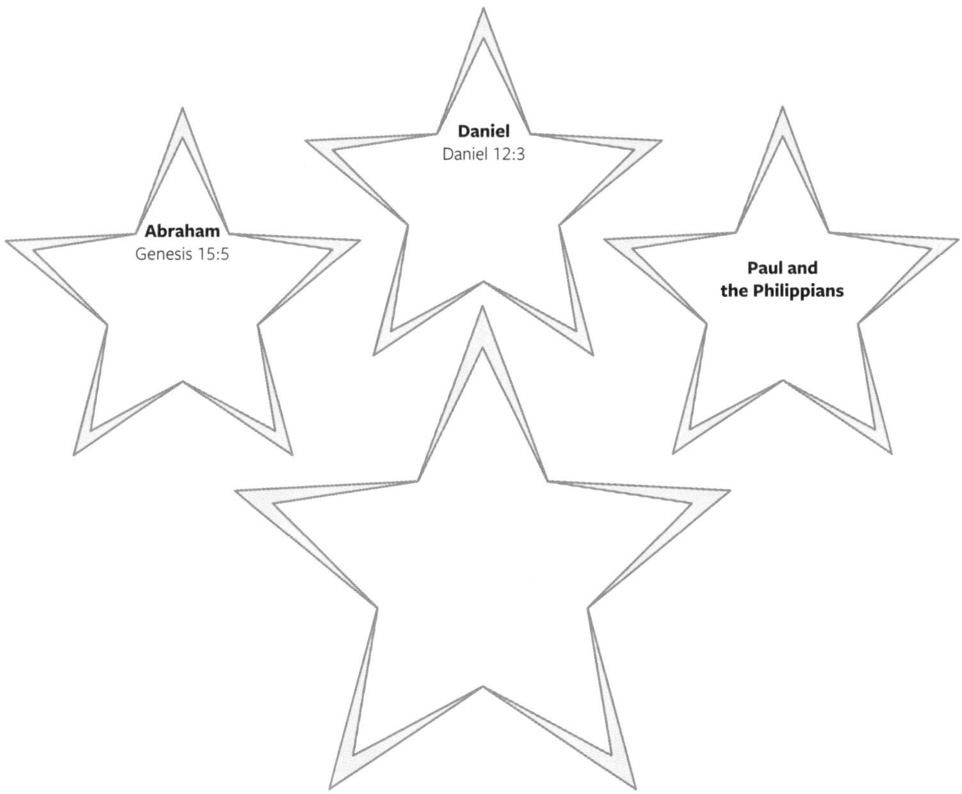

Throughout the history of God's people, Scripture sings: *"Don't look to your circumstances—look to the one who made the stars."* God asked Abraham to trust His promise that he'd have a child, even though he "was as good as dead" (Romans 4:19). God put it on Daniel's heart to do things His way, even if it meant being thrown into a pit of lions (Daniel 6:16). Paul already illustrated how Jesus poured Himself out even unto death on a cross and God raised Him up (Philippians 2:8). These stories give us hope and encouragement (Romans 4:23–24).

Review 2:16–18.

Lest you think 2:16 was Paul telling the Philippians, *"Do this so I look good,"* check out the verse that follows. The "drink offering" in 2:17 alludes to the pouring out of wine on animal sacrifices. Paul was willing to die for the sake of their faith. He was reminding them of what was on the line as they persevered without grumbling: Those who suffered and died that they might have faith didn't do so in vain.

That principle helps us understand 2:18. Paul wasn't asking the Philippians to be happy about death. Even Jesus wept when Lazarus died. We can hate death—it is evidence of the world's brokenness and man's fallen nature. But Paul invited the Philippians to "be glad and rejoice with [him]" because of what that pouring out would produce.

Abraham believed. Then Daniel believed. Then Paul believed. Then the Philippians believed. And now, you in your generation believe. And you will shine.

3. In the fourth star above, write a prayer that God would strengthen you to cast off grumbling that you might shine like stars in the universe.

DAY 4

Philippians 2:19–24

READ PHILIPPIANS 2:19–24

Review 2:19–22.

On Days 1–3, Paul encouraged the Philippians to walk out their faith with the mind of Christ, pouring themselves out as He did. Now on Days 4–5, Paul was basically saying, *"Speaking of all these things, here are two great human examples. I'm sending them to you."*

Paul expected to be encouraged by the news Timothy would bring back, because this Philippian church was a church he deeply loved and had been encouraged by. Throughout this letter, he thanked and praised them: *"You're doing a great job—keep it up!"*

Timothy lived in Lystra and joined up with Paul during his second missionary journey (Acts 16:1–4). He was the grandson of Lois and the son of Eunice—two women Paul credited as having a sincerity of faith they passed on to Timothy (2 Timothy 1:5).

1. What did Paul say about Timothy in this passage?

   A. He's okay with me.

   B. He's one of many faithful servants I trust.

   C. I have no one like him.

   D. He betrayed me, but I have forgiven him.

Paul knew Timothy would care for the Philippians as he himself would. Typically, people seek their own interests, but Paul said Timothy had proven otherwise. Remember, in the opening of this letter (1:1), Paul referred to himself and Timothy equally as servants. He thought of Timothy as a co-laborer. And Paul even called Timothy a son—they had a special bond. But this also points to a larger theme Paul exhibited throughout his ministry: Despite often being imprisoned, there was nothing isolated about him. He was constantly rejoicing in collaboration, modeling humility, and bringing others in.

★ 2. Are there areas of your life where you've seen this done well, or where you've been a beneficiary of this kind of co-laboring? If not, are there any areas where you could prayerfully help initiate that kind of relationship? In either case, describe.

3. Write a prayer about any areas where you feel resistant to co-laboring. Some challenges to pray over might include: "I don't trust anyone to do it like I do it." "I hate delegating." "I've been burned in the past." "I don't know where to begin—no one wants me to be involved." Ask God to speak truth over any lies that would keep you from the joy, fellowship, and victories He has waiting for you in community. Don't miss them!

Review 2:23–24.

As Paul expressed in 1:19–23, he didn't know whether he would live or die, but he spoke of the future openhandedly. He was willing to be interrupted according to God's will, and he let all his plans remain subject to God. But Paul hoped he could send Timothy soon—and that he could come himself shortly afterward.

★ 4. On a scale of one to ten, how openhanded are you with your plans for the future? See James 4:13–16 for more insight.

1 2 3 4 5 6 7 8 9 10

DAY 5

Philippians 2:25–30

READ PHILIPPIANS 2:25–30

Review 2:25.

Epaphroditus was likely the one who delivered this letter to the Philippian church, as well as financial gifts to Paul (4:18). He was both a messenger and a minister to need—but Paul also referred to him in three other ways.

1. Match Paul's description of Epaphroditus to its application.

Brother	with Paul in work
Fellow worker	with Paul in battle
Fellow soldier	with Paul in relationship

These descriptions seem to escalate in commitment.

★ 2. Do you have any relationships that go all the way to togetherness in battle? Briefly describe.

Review 2:26–30.

Paul knew the Philippians were worried about Epaphroditus, but he wanted them to know Epaphroditus was okay. He almost died, but God had mercy and spared his life—and also Paul's heart. The beauty of this relationship was so straightforward. These weren't just coworkers doing a job; their hearts were with each other. Intimacy marked every part of this early church's life: shared sufferings, shared finances, shared hopes, shared endeavors.

★ 3. Does this challenge your idea of privacy? Do you view yourself as more of a "giver" who doesn't need anything from others? Or can you rightly see yourself as someone who needs the ministry of others? Why do you think God designed us to have those needs?

Note there's nothing in this passage that implies Epaphroditus's recovery was miraculous, but Paul still saw God's hand in it.

Paul was eager to send Epaphroditus so the Philippians could see for themselves that he was well, though he'd nearly died to complete "what was lacking" in their service. This phrase could refer to physical distance that kept them from supporting Paul or a gap in their financial support due to their own hardship. Whatever the case, Paul praised the Philippians for their support and encouragement to him throughout this letter. And all the more, he praised Epaphroditus for going the extra mile to fill in the gap.

God continually provided for Paul in the gaps during his ministry. And God's provision often came through the willingness of others to step in. But His provision wasn't only financial.

How encouraging it must've been to Paul—who himself had so often faced risk of death and illness, chains and imprisonment—to see someone else running to battle *with him*. God provided friendship for Paul, people who said, *"I'm with you . . . even unto death."*

We don't need to *seek* death. But where might our friendships look more like Paul's—whatever may come?

4. Who said, "Greater love has no one than this, that someone lay down his life for his friends" (John 15:13)? And when?

Jesus is where the *best* friendship is. And He's where the joy is!

5. What stood out to you most in this week's study? Why?

6. What did you learn or relearn about God and His character this week?

DAY 6

Corresponding Psalm & Prayer

READ PSALM 8

1. What correlation do you see between Psalm 8 and this week's study?

2. What portions of this psalm stand out to you most?

3. Close by praying this prayer aloud:

Father,

When I look at Your heavens, the work of Your fingers, the moon and the stars, which You have set in place, who am I that You are mindful of me?

You are merciful, but I've tried to work for my own salvation. You are gracious, but I've sought my own interests. When my brothers and sisters were in need, I sometimes refused to give help. When I was in need, I sometimes refused to accept help. I've grumbled. I've disputed. And I repent.

Like Paul encouraged the Philippians to do, help me to think rightly of You. Help me to think rightly of myself. Help me become more like You. And in doing so, may I shine like stars in the universe—the very stars You made!

I surrender my life to You, Lord—every moment of my day, each decision I make, I yield my will and way to Your perfect will and way.

I love You too. Amen.

DAY 7

Rest, Catch Up, or Dig Deeper

WEEKLY CHALLENGE

In Day 3, Paul encouraged the Philippians to "do all things without grumbling or disputing" that in "a crooked and depraved generation . . . [they might] shine as lights in the world" (2:14–15). This week, aim to eliminate grumbling and complaining from your words and even your thoughts. This will likely be more challenging than you can imagine. It might be helpful to write Philippians 4:8 on a three-by-five-inch card or set it as your phone wallpaper to help you remember what you should be thinking (and talking) about instead.

WEEK 4

Philippians 3

Scripture to Memorize

Therefore God has highly exalted him and bestowed on him the name that is above every name . . .

Philippians 2:9

DAILY BIBLE READING

Day 1: Philippians 3:1
Day 2: Philippians 3:2–7
Day 3: Philippians 3:8–11
Day 4: Philippians 3:12–16
Day 5: Philippians 3:17–21
Day 6: Psalm 18
Day 7: Catch-Up Day

Corresponds to Day 351 of *The Bible Recap.*

WEEKLY CHALLENGE

See page 91 for more information.

DAY 1

Philippians 3:1

READ PHILIPPIANS 3:1

This section's first word, *finally*, usually signals the end of a message. It sounds as though Paul were wrapping up his letter, saying, "*In conclusion . . .*" However, his Greek audience would have understood this to be an introductory word more along the lines of *furthermore*.[1] In fact, his tone was about to shift to address something the saints in Philippi needed to be on guard against.

But first: Rejoice!

Review 3:1a.

This wasn't a call to manufacture joy or put on a happy face. His reminder to them was to rejoice *in the Lord*.

Paul knew that circumstances, whether good or bad, couldn't produce lasting joy. He didn't want the saints to be under any illusion that true joy was an internal response to living "the good life" or having worldly prosperity. He was familiar with the reality of pain and suffering. He was in prison, after all! But when things felt unsteady, he knew Jesus was constant.

★ 1. How does this inform your view of joy? Based on what you know about Jesus, what makes Him a reliable source of joy?

Review 3:1b.

2. Look back at what you've read so far, or use a lexicon or concordance to help you research. How many times have you seen the words *rejoice* and *joy* so far in this letter?

Paul knew he was repeating himself. But he wasn't being condescending. He knew that humans are a forgetful lot. We're also prone to complaining and negativity. Paul knew how vital it was for them to remember to rejoice in Christ as they sought to grow in maturity.

★ 3. Why might rejoicing in Christ strengthen your faith?

Review 3:1b one more time.

4. What reason does Paul give for repeating himself?

This mention of "safety" signaled an interesting shift in Paul's tone. With a letter that focused almost entirely on encouragement, you can almost picture his audience thinking, *Safety? Who said anything about danger? Should we be concerned?*

Tomorrow, we'll see three areas that deeply concerned Paul and posed a threat to this church's joy.

DAY 2

Philippians 3:2–7

READ PHILIPPIANS 3:2–7

Review 3:2.

Paul will return to the topic of rejoicing later in his letter, but here he offered a strong warning about those who sought to rob the Philippians of the joy of their salvation. Those who challenged the gospel were part of a religious faction known as the Judaizers.

1. **Look up the term *Judaizers* using a web search or a Bible dictionary.** How did their message oppose the true gospel?

Jesus reserved His most forceful language for the Pharisees, because they heaped heavy burdens on people for keeping the law as a means of righteousness (Matthew 23). In the same way, Paul vehemently opposed those who challenged the gospel of Christ—each word choice hitting harder than the last.

2. What three descriptors did Paul give to those who challenged the gospel?

3. Using a Bible study tool, explain why the word *dogs* would've been especially insulting to the Judaizers.

"Evildoers" likely alluded to their claim that righteousness came from works. Here, Paul was exposing their true colors: Only evil workers would draw people away from the free gift of salvation. Paul's final label, "those who mutilate the flesh," carried a meaning that gets a bit lost in our English translation—one that would have sent the Judaizers reeling.

The Greek word for circumcision was *peritomē*. But Paul replaced *peritomē* with *katatomē*—a pagan practice of flesh mutilation. There was nothing wrong with circumcision itself. But these dogs, these evildoers, had turned it into a requirement for salvation—which was nothing short of heresy.

Anything that adds a requirement for salvation outside of placing your faith in Jesus is heresy (Romans 10:9–10). There's nothing you can do to add to your salvation—to help accomplish or maintain it (Ephesians 2:8–9). Jesus didn't die so that you'd keep striving for God's acceptance.

★ 4. Have you ever thought you had to do something to gain or maintain God's approval? If so, how are these verses an encouragement to you?

Review 3:3–6.

Christ-followers—those who worship in the Spirit of God—are the only true circumcision, the true members of God's family. Paul doubled down by saying, "We . . . put no confidence in the flesh."

Paul said that if anyone had reason to believe they could put confidence in their flesh, it was him. Before you think this sounds arrogant, wait to see what Paul thinks of his "pedigree."

5. Paul lists seven ways he would have checked all the religious boxes. Write them and what made them notable below. The first one has been done for you.

Qualification	What made this notable?
Circumcised on the eighth day	*Showed that he was Jewish from birth—not a convert later in life*

Review 3:7.

Where the world might have put Paul among the religious elite—the *most* righteous—Paul counted these so-called gains as loss. He had experienced a total role reversal. He saw this list and knew it had gotten him *exactly nowhere* in respect to righteousness.

For Paul, the only real gain in life was being found in Christ.

DAY 3

Philippians 3:8–11

READ PHILIPPIANS 3:8–11

After listing his religious résumé, Paul essentially threw it in the trash. He knew that none of his past accomplishments held any value. But it wasn't just his past that needed to be tossed.

Review 3:8.

Paul not only counted his past as a Pharisee as loss, he counted *everything* as loss compared to Christ. Notice that he didn't refer to these things as second compared to Christ—he said they're *worthless* compared to Christ. Paul lost a lot when he followed Jesus. It's safe to assume he lost relationships, respect, and positions of power. Everything about his life shifted.

Isn't it interesting that we never hear Paul speak *fondly* of those things? We never hear him complain about what following Jesus cost him in his personal life. And it's because knowing Christ was so much better than anything he'd ever experienced before.

★ 1. How has your life changed since you came to Christ? How does experiencing the love of Christ compare to what your life was like before?

Your Bible likely uses the word *rubbish* or *garbage* in this verse. Paul's actual word here in the Greek suggests something much more crass—it wasn't exactly dinner table conversation. It's not that Paul hated his heritage or even the story of his past—it's just that when you pit those things against the "surpassing worth" of knowing Christ, there is no comparison to the joy and light He brings.

Review 3:9–11.

Paul took his audience on a succinct journey through the Christian life: our justification, sanctification, and glorification. Let's zoom in on what he's teaching them. It's important for us to understand these terms and to see them in our story.

2. **Using a Bible dictionary, define the following terms in one or two sentences.**

Justification:

Sanctification:

Glorification:

3. Now, using the phrases from Paul's letter, match each one with their appropriate term. Hint: Some terms have multiple answers.

- Attain the resurrection from the dead
- To know Him and His power
- To share in His sufferings
- Having righteousness from faith in Christ
- To become like Him
- Being found in Him

- Justification
- Sanctification
- Glorification

Our righteousness is based on faith in *Christ's* finished works—not our own (justification). Once we are *in Christ*, we'll experience suffering as the old things pass away, but we can rejoice in this suffering because it's making us more like Jesus (sanctification). And the Spirit empowers us until we are united with Christ in our death or upon His return (glorification).

Now, let's zoom out and apply this to the journey of our lives.

4. Using the timeline below, label how each of these concepts plays out in the life of the believer.

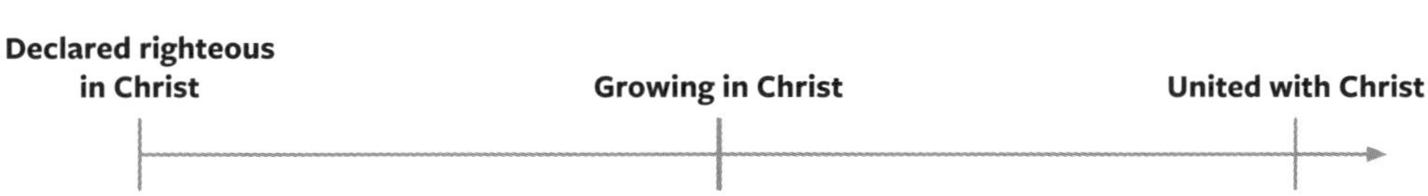

____________ ____________ ____________

In your daily life, recall "the power of His resurrection." This truth is an invitation to utilize power that's available to you *now*. There *will* be a resurrection from the dead, and we *will* be glorified when we see Jesus. But right now, as you go about your day, remember that Christ's resurrection power is at work mightily in your life!

DAY 4

Philippians 3:12–16

READ PHILIPPIANS 3:12–16

Yesterday, we identified the process of sanctification—our journey between justification and glorification. As Paul continued his letter, he leveled the playing field between himself and his beloved congregation in Philippi. It's as if he were saying, *"Don't misunderstand! God's still working on me too."*

Review 3:12.

1. What did Paul mean by his first statement? What had he not already obtained?

Many believers are quick to compare themselves to others. We look around and see others running the race, and when we feel they're leaving us in the dust, we tend to feel shame. Or worse yet, we want to quit running altogether.

Paul set the example for what to do when we realize we have not yet arrived: *We press on*. But it's important to note that Paul wasn't telling the Philippians to press on and strive *for salvation*. On the contrary, he was reminding them that sanctification was about living a life congruent with a position they *already had* in Christ. We press on to find even more of Christ's "unsearchable riches" (Ephesians 3:8).

Review 3:13–14.

★ 2. What two actions did Paul say he would take to reach perfection? (Hint: He defined the two actions as the "one thing" he must do.) Which of these is more difficult for you?

To keep this in context, remember that Paul had just told them how worthless his past achievements were. But everyone's journey is different. What might be holding *you* back from growing in Christ?

3. Ask God to examine your heart. Is there anything holding you back? Is it self-righteousness? Is it comparison? Is there sin that keeps you from joyfully and ambitiously striving toward the upward call? If God brings anything to mind, write a prayer asking Him to remove this obstacle.

Knowing that he hadn't yet reached perfection, Paul repeated this phrase from 3:12: "I press on." This isn't a passive form of trudging along, and it doesn't indicate a runner barely dragging their feet across the finish line. This was a phrase the Greeks used "to describe a hunter eagerly pursuing his prey."[1]

★ 4. There is some debate over exactly what this "prize of the upward call" is that Paul referred to. Based on the three terms we learned yesterday (about the lifetime of a believer), what do you think Paul meant? Use a Bible study tool to support your answer.

Review 3:15–16.

One of the clearest signs of maturity is knowing you have room to grow. Paul assured the Philippians they could do this the easy way or they could do it the hard way. But if they became complacent, thinking they had already achieved perfection, God would set them straight.

Philippians 3:16 in the New Living Translation says, "We must hold on to the progress we have already made." We're all in various stages in our journey of sanctification, and there's much we don't yet know. But we, setting our sights on the prize, must be determined to finish the race set before us!

DAY 5

Philippians 3:17–21

READ PHILIPPIANS 3:17–21

Review 3:17.

Lest we think Paul has let his righteousness go to his head, let's remember how he has described himself so far in this letter: he is a servant of Christ Jesus (1:1), he attributes all glory and praise to God (1:11), both his life and his death are for the sake of Christ (1:20), and his hope is in the Lord Jesus (2:19).

1. What else in this letter points to Paul's humility? Why do you think Paul told them to imitate *him* (see 1 Corinthians 11:1 for help)?

We all need to surround ourselves with people who encourage, challenge, and lead us. We're easily influenced and distracted, so keeping company with those who are "pressing on toward the upward call" is crucial to our growth.

★ 2. Why is it important to set a Christlike example? Is there someone you know who looks up to you and watches how you act? How closely does what they see resemble Christ?

Review 3:18–19.

Paul was likely describing either the Judaizers we learned about on Day 2 or rebels who essentially lived however they wanted. Paul's descriptions actually fit both. His warning could have been about falling into legalism *or* licentiousness. Both brought Paul great sorrow.

★ 3. **Look up the definitions for these two words.** Which one do you have a stronger tendency to fall into?

Legalism:

Licentiousness:

It's important to note that Paul considered both camps to be "enemies of the cross." This is something we must take seriously. If you tend toward legalism, then you act as though Jesus died in vain *and* you miss out on the joy of freedom in Christ. If you tend toward licentiousness, then you make a mockery of all Jesus endured for you *and* you miss out on the beauty of obedience.

Review 3:20.

When we studied 1:27–28, we learned about the status and power that came from being a Roman citizen. It was a prestigious privilege, and many took it on as their personal identity. And part of that identity was recognizing Caesar as "lord." In fact, "in 48 B.C. Julius Caesar was declared to be the 'universal savior of mankind.'"[1]

All of this is what made Paul's statement so countercultural. Dangerous, even. For Christians, our citizenship is in heaven. And we have one Savior: the Lord Jesus Christ.

Review 3:21.

This is the hope set before us. No matter how painful, disordered, and unjust life may feel now, we can set our sights on heaven and on our Savior, who will set all things right. This is why even during imprisonment, Paul could rejoice in Christ—because He's where the joy is.

4. What stood out to you most in this week's study? Why?

5. What did you learn or relearn about God and His character this week?

DAY 6

Corresponding Psalm & Prayer

READ PSALM 18

1. What correlation do you see between Psalm 18 and this week's study?

2. What portions of this psalm stand out to you most?

3. Close by praying this prayer aloud:

Father,

We worship by the Spirit, we glory in the Son, and we rejoice in You. Salvation belongs to You, and You alone are worthy to be praised!

But I'm forgetful—of Your worthiness and so much more. Like the Israelites, I'm prone to complaining and negativity. Like the Judaizers, I've added my own requirements to Your gospel—for others and for myself. And God, I repent. Every rule I've tried to impose on my brothers and sisters—it's garbage. Every deed I've done to try to earn my own salvation—it's rubbish. Jesus, You didn't die so that I would keep striving for Your acceptance. Forgive me.

When I do what appears right, but for the wrong reasons, remind me that You have already paid for my justification. When I do what looks good, but with bad intentions, remind me that You are actively working for my sanctification. And when I fear the unknowns ahead of me, remind me that You await me with the unimaginable riches of my glorification. As You make me more like You—no matter what comes—help me press on.

Grant me the joy of freedom and the beauty of obedience. I surrender my life to You, Lord—every moment of my day, each decision I make, I yield my will and way to Your perfect will and way.

I love You too. Amen.

DAY 7

Rest, Catch Up, or Dig Deeper

WEEKLY CHALLENGE

On Day 5, Paul encouraged the Philippians to imitate him as an example of following Christ. Could you say the same? This week, pay attention to your actions and words and evaluate whether you could encourage someone to come behind you and imitate your actions as they strive to imitate Christ.

WEEK 5

Philippians 4

Scripture to Memorize

. . . so that at the name of Jesus every knee should bow, in heaven and on earth and under the earth, and every tongue confess that Jesus Christ is Lord, to the glory of God the Father.

Philippians 2:10–11

DAILY BIBLE READING

Day 1: Philippians 4:1–3

Day 2: Philippians 4:4–9

Day 3: Philippians 4:10–13

Day 4: Philippians 4:14–20

Day 5: Philippians 4:21–23

Day 6: Psalm 100

Day 7: Catch-Up Day

Corresponds to Day 351 of *The Bible Recap.*

WEEKLY CHALLENGE

See page 110 for more information.

DAY 1

Philippians 4:1–3

READ PHILIPPIANS 4:1–3

Review 4:1.

As Paul began to wrap up his letter, he emphasized once again the mutual love and friendship between himself and the Philippian church. He considered them not only his brothers and sisters in Christ but also his "joy and crown." This statement most likely had both present and future implications for Paul. The Philippians' steadfast faith and partnership in the gospel brought him joy in his immediate circumstances, and it would also be his reward when Christ returned.

1. Reread 1:27 and find the phrase that is repeated in 4:1. Write it below. Based on what you've learned so far, why do you think Paul repeated it?

Review 4:2–3.

Did you notice that Paul didn't mention what was going on between these two women? Maybe there was an important decision they needed to make, maybe they had a disagreement, or maybe this was about something else entirely. Paul clearly didn't see the need to include specifics. They would have known what he was referring to; so while we can speculate, it's better to focus on Paul's main point—urging these women to "agree in the Lord."

The tone here was encouraging and exhorting rather than rebuking or commanding. Paul's request was for unity between these female co-laborers—the same kind of unity he encouraged the whole church to exhibit throughout his letter. The phrase translated here as "agree in the Lord" can also be translated "be of the same mind."

★ 2. Reread 2:2 and 2:5. What connection do you see between these verses and Paul's exhortation in 4:2? How does that help you understand Paul's exhortation to these women?

3. **Using a commentary, look up 4:3 and see what it says about the phrase "true companion."** Write down what you find. Why do you think it's significant that Paul requested their help? Explain.

Paul ended this section with a reminder of the unity all believers share: Their names were *already* written in the Book of Life (Luke 10:20; Revelation 3:5, 13:8) and would never be removed! This was a reminder in the midst of a situation that was either already bringing disunity or had the possibility to bring disunity that they were all on the same team. And they had a noble and high call: to have and demonstrate the mind of Christ as ones whose names were already written in His book.

★ 4. Has your view of unity or agreement in the Lord changed? Explain.

DAY 2

Philippians 4:4–9

READ PHILIPPIANS 4:4–9

Review 4:4.

Paul commanded the Philippians once again to rejoice—two times in just one verse. He even emphasized the fact that he was repeating himself. Paul took rejoicing seriously!

1. Have you been encouraged or challenged by the theme of rejoicing in Philippians? If so, explain.

Review 4:5–7.

The word *reasonableness* highlights the theme we studied yesterday and in 2:1–5: having the same mind, agreeing in the Lord. Paul called the Philippians to live out this gentleness, humility, and forbearance for the world to see.

It's debated whether the phrase "the Lord is at hand" refers to 4:5 or 4:6. Paul might have encouraged the Philippians to live reasonably and humbly because they were anticipating Christ's return. Or this phrase could refer to the closeness of the Lord's presence, therefore saying, *"Don't be anxious, because He's near."*[1]

Or what if it's both? The truth is, Jesus is coming back—and that reality should impact our witness to the world. *And* Jesus is near, so we don't have to be anxious about anything.

★ 2. Do you live as if "the Lord is at hand"? Why or why not?

Paul makes a bold statement—a command—literally translated "be anxious for nothing." Being in prison when he wrote this, Paul had no idea what was going to happen to him or what his earthly future looked like. You might be thinking, *How can he possibly say not to be anxious?* His answer was simple yet profound: rejoicing, prayer, and a mind focused on worthy things.

Paul used four different words to describe how prayer was—and still is—the appropriate response to anxiety. *Prayer* is the most common word used for communication with God and can refer to talking to God about anything. *Supplication* refers to a more urgent expression of a need, and Paul combined this with *thanksgiving*. Gratitude focuses on the faithfulness of God, including the ways He's answered prayers before. And finally, *requests* describe all the things you ask for in prayer.

3. Summarize 4:7 in your own words. What is the result of this multifaceted prayer?

Review 4:8.

Paul listed eight things that should characterize the thoughts filling the Philippians' minds—and ours too. Reading through this list gives us good targets for where to aim our thoughts. For example: *What's true?* God is with you. *What's honorable?* Those who serve in unseen positions in the church.

★ 4. Pick three words from 4:8 and find something in your life that fits into those categories. Write one to two sentences about each of the three things you picked, then thank God for them!

Review 4:9.

It's important to remember that Paul wasn't superhuman. He certainly had moments of fear, anxiety, shame, depression, and dread. And his expectation and hope for the beloved Philippian church wasn't that they would be perfect—it was that they would *practice*.

The Philippians knew the truth, and they had already been following Paul's example. Yet he reminded them to repeatedly and habitually put all these things into practice—again and again.

Let this be an encouragement to you. As you battle anxiety through prayer and set your mind on true, praiseworthy things, you're following the example of *practice*, not perfection. There might be harder days, and there might be prayers that feel monotonous. But the God of peace will be with you, just as He was with Paul and the Philippians.

DAY 3

Philippians 4:10–13

READ PHILIPPIANS 4:10–13

Review 4:10.

One final time, Paul rejoiced in the Lord, this time because the Philippians had sent him a gift. It seems the Philippians had wanted to express their appreciation and partnership with Paul for a while, but there hadn't been an opportunity. Paul's imprisonment created an occasion for them to provide financially for some, or perhaps even all, of his needs.

The word translated "concerned" is the same word Paul used throughout his letter to speak about "being of the same mind." The Philippians' gift represented their humble, selfless attitude—the very thing Paul was encouraging them to live out. No wonder he rejoiced!

★ 1. Write the name of a church, ministry, mentor, or brother or sister in Christ who has impacted your life. Brainstorm a few ways you could express your "concern" for them.

Review 4:11–12.

Although Paul was thanking the Philippians, he also wanted them to know that despite his situation, he was content—with or without their donation.

2. Fill in the blanks in 4:11 below.

"I have ______________ in __________________ situation I am to be ________________."

Over the years, Paul had learned the discipline of contentment. It wasn't just miraculously granted to him during his imprisonment in Rome. Through abundance and poverty, in danger and in peace, he practiced and developed this skill. But lest you feel overwhelmed or discouraged in your own journey of contentment, remember the *source* of Paul's, and our, peace.

Review 4:13.

This is a popular verse—one you've likely seen on T-shirts, on coffee mugs, or at your favorite sporting event. However, putting it back into the original context provides a greater depth of understanding.

Greek philosophy viewed contentment through the lens of self-sufficiency.[1] This might have been the mindset of some of the Philippians before their conversion. Self-sufficiency and self-seeking attitudes permeate our day as well—promising power, love, and peace if we just buy more, fix ourselves, and take control.

But you can never be the source of your own contentment. Instead, Christians rely on the sufficiency of Christ. He is the one who strengthens us to *endure* all things. Paul experienced this "Christ-sufficiency" empowering him to be content in times of both abundance and lack.[2] And Christ will certainly do the same for you as you lean into Him.

★ 3. Write down a few areas where you struggle to be content—whether in abundance or in areas of need. Pray for contentment, knowing Christ Himself strengthens you.

DAY 4

Philippians 4:14–20

READ PHILIPPIANS 4:14–20

Review 4:14.

Make no mistake, Paul was thankful for the Philippians' financial gift. Although he was content no matter the circumstances, he appreciated his friends' active partnership in ministry.

Review 4:15–16.

1. Circle any churches that financially supported Paul.

   A. Thessalonica

   B. Corinth and Galatia

   C. Ephesus

   D. Philippi

   E. All of the above

Paul reviewed his shared history with the Philippians. From the very beginning, the Philippians' minds were focused on gospel partnership, and they expressed this through their generosity. After establishing the Philippian church in the region of Macedonia, Paul stopped in Thessalonica (Acts 17:1). And even though he had just been with the Philippians, they quickly sent him a gift as he ministered in a new location.

Review 4:17–18.

Paul was grateful for the Philippians' help in supplying his needs, but he was more excited about what the gift represented and the way it would benefit his friends. The Philippians' generosity overflowed from the maturity of their faith and their willingness to sacrifice for the advancement of the gospel. Paul was certain this would lead to blessings and reward for them—whether physical or spiritual, immediate or future. Paul ultimately saw their gift as a sacrifice to the Lord.

2. Look up the verses in the table below and compare them with 4:18. Write down the similar phrases.

Ephesians 5:2	
Leviticus 1:9	
Romans 12:2	

★ 3. Why do you think Paul used Old Testament sacrificial language to describe the Philippians' financial support?

Review 4:19–20.

Paul experienced miraculous provision with the arrival of Epaphroditus and the gifts. Paul saw God provide for him, and he was confident that God's unlimited resources would be available for His other children too. Paul wanted the Philippians to know that their needs would *also* be met out of God's abundance.

★ 4. Think back on a time when you saw God provide for your needs—physical, spiritual, emotional, et cetera. How did that experience give you more confidence in God's continual provision for you? Explain.

The reality of God's lavish and infinite resources led Paul to a place of worship. Despite imprisonment, Paul was content. In the midst of the unknown, he rejoiced. God's abundance was clear in Paul's life, and He had already supplied all Paul needed. And to that Paul said, "Amen."

DAY 5

Philippians 4:21–23

READ PHILIPPIANS 4:21–23

Review 4:21a.

Paul's final greeting mirrors the beginning of his letter, calling the Philippians "saints in Christ Jesus" (1:1). As a reminder, *saints* is a general term for all believers. It can also mean "holy" or "set-apart ones."

1. How have you seen Paul encourage the Philippians to be "set apart" throughout this letter? What attitudes and behaviors did he highlight? Include chapter-and-verse references in your answers.

★ 2. Based on your study, what are some ways God might be calling you to be "set apart"?

Review 4:21b–22.

Two groups of people sent their greetings to the Philippian church. "The brothers" most likely included Timothy and Epaphroditus, as well as other co-laborers in Rome. "All the saints" referred to the rest of the Roman Christians, and Paul highlighted a unique subgroup: "Caesar's household."

In 1:12–14, you learned that Paul's imprisonment had led to some soldiers in the Roman military hearing the gospel. Here it's clear that the good news had also made its way to Caesar's palace (not the one in Vegas)! It's likely those in Caesar's house included slaves, family members, and even government employees. Both the lowly and influential were responding to the gospel message.

Saints in Caesar's household might have seemed like an impossibility. *Caesar* was lord in his household, not Christ. And although the Roman mindset generally had no problem adding new gods to their worship, the exclusive worship of the *true* Lord, Jesus Christ, was outside of the typical Roman citizen's comfort zone. Yet nothing can stop the power of the gospel of Jesus Christ! There were saints—people set apart for God—in Caesar's household, and they sent their greetings to their fellow brothers and sisters in Philippi.

★ 3. Is it hard to believe that God is at work in the secular spaces around you or in the world? How does the presence of saints in Caesar's household encourage you? Explain.

Review 4:23.

Paul's life was shaped by the grace of God, and he wanted the Philippians to know the presence of this grace deep within their inner being ("spirit"). The unmerited favor found only in and through Jesus Christ sustained Paul. The grace of Jesus helped him write a letter full of rejoicing to his dear friends in Philippi. Paul's letter served to remind them—and us—that He's where the joy is!

4. What stood out to you most in this week's study? Why?

5. What did you learn or relearn about God and His character this week?

DAY 6

Corresponding Psalm & Prayer

READ PSALM 100

1. What correlation do you see between Psalm 100 and this week's study?

2. What portions of this psalm stand out to you most?

3. Close by praying this prayer aloud:

Father,

You are the Lord, and You are God! You are good, and I give thanks to You. Your steadfast love endures forever, and I bless Your name. You are faithful through all generations, and still to me. I am Yours—a sheep in Your pasture.

God, You have made me a saint, but I'm also a sinner, and I repent of my sins. Sometimes out of fear and sometimes out of doubt, I've ignored Your invitation to better thoughts. I've not only thought about things that are false, dishonorable, unjust, filthy, and unlovely, but dwelled on them, and with my words and actions, I've invited others to dwell on them too. Forgive me.

Purify my mind, Lord. Let me dwell on things that are true, honorable, just, pure, and lovely. Help me strive for unity with my brothers and sisters in my local church, and multiply our efforts. Help the global church to stand firm in You and to flourish. May we be beautifully diverse and supernaturally united. Remind us that You are at hand—You're coming soon, and in the meantime, You're near.

No matter what comes, I rely on You to be my sufficiency. You alone give me strength. I surrender my life to You, Lord—every moment of my day, each decision I make, I yield my will and way to Your perfect will and way.

I love You too. Amen.

DAY 7

Rest, Catch Up, or Dig Deeper

WEEKLY CHALLENGE

On Day 2, Paul told the Philippians to "be anxious for nothing" (NKJV) and to *replace* their worries and anxieties with prayer. This week, make two lists.

List 1: Things you're inclined to worry or feel anxious about

List 2: Things you're grateful for (including situations where you saw God's faithfulness)

Spend ten minutes praying from your lists every day. When you feel anxious this week, commit to bringing that thought or situation directly to God in prayer. Remember, this is about *practice*, so you may have to remind yourself to return to prayer as anxious thoughts come up.

INTRODUCTION TO COLOSSIANS

Paul's letter to the Colossians is quite different from his letter to the Philippians, and it will be helpful to understand why as you begin studying. Though Paul cared deeply for this body of believers, he never actually met them in person. The church in Colossae is believed to have been founded by a man named Epaphras, probably after he encountered Paul and his message in Ephesus (Acts 19). As an enthusiastic new believer, Epaphras took the message of the gospel to Colossae, which is now in Turkey.

The population in Colossae was mostly Gentile and pagan, though there was a moderate number of Jewish people. This led to a unique culture in the church there, and unfortunately it also led to heresy seeping into the church. This heresy included both a hyper-legalistic view of the Hebrew law and a mystical "higher knowledge" that denied the deity of Christ. Epaphras did his best to shepherd this flock, and when he visited the imprisoned Paul in Rome, he talked about his concerns with Paul. Their conversations prompted this letter.

Paul wrote Colossians around the same time as Philippians: AD 60–62. He also intended for this letter to be shared with Colossae's neighbor, Laodicea. Paul wanted his spiritual brothers and sisters to understand and submit to the preeminence and sufficiency of Christ. The first half of the letter is doctrinal, explaining why Christ is preeminent and sufficient. The second half of the letter is practical, explaining how the Colossians should submit to Him.

You'll come across a name that may feel familiar as you study; Philemon was a member of the church in Colossae, and he got his very own letter from Paul, which was also canonized in the New Testament.

Now let's dig into what the book of Colossians has to say.

WEEK 6

Colossians 1:1–14

Scripture to Memorize

He is the image of the invisible God, the firstborn of all creation.

Colossians 1:15

DAILY BIBLE READING

Day 1: Colossians 1:1–2

Day 2: Colossians 1:3–5a

Day 3: Colossians 1:5b–8

Day 4: Colossians 1:9–10

Day 5: Colossians 1:11–14

Day 6: Psalm 33

Day 7: Catch-Up Day

Corresponds to Day 349 of *The Bible Recap.*

WEEKLY CHALLENGE

See page 131 for more information.

DAY 1

Colossians 1:1–2

READ COLOSSIANS 1:1–2

Review 1:1.

Paul began this letter to the church in Colossae by immediately identifying himself as the author. While he never actually visited the city of Colossae, the timing of his letter was crucial to the health of this particular church. The truths he shared with them were fundamental to Christian doctrine and are still vital for us today.

★ 1. **Use a Bible study tool to find the definition of *apostle* and write it below.** Why might this be an important distinction for Paul to make about himself?

2. How was Paul appointed as an apostle?

The believers in Colossae had heard the gospel because of a man named Epaphras, whom we'll meet later. And while Paul was a spiritual grandfather to the Colossians, they didn't know him personally. It was important for them to know that this message from Paul was a message from God Himself.

Timothy wasn't an apostle, but he was a brother in the faith. He faithfully ministered to Paul in prison and served alongside him in Rome.

Review 1:2.

Paul used the term *saints* in many of his letters. Again, this wasn't a special distinction of superiority. As we learned in our study of Philippians, *saints* simply refers to all Christians. Paul's description of the saints as "faithful brothers" alluded to their positive reputation. The word used for *brothers* here (*adelphos*) referred to both men and women in the church.

There's more than meets the eye in Paul's opening sentences. Twice, he identified Jesus using the word *Christ*. Contrary to what you might have once thought, Christ was not Jesus's last name.

3. **Look up the term *Christ* and write its definition and/or synonym below.**

It's easy to miss the significance of this. For *centuries*, God's people had been watching and waiting for the Savior to come. The true Savior. Right out of the gate, Paul took a stance: Jesus was not merely a man—*He is the Christ*. This will be an important theme throughout the rest of this letter.

4. To get your bearings for this part of the study, circle Colossae on the map below.

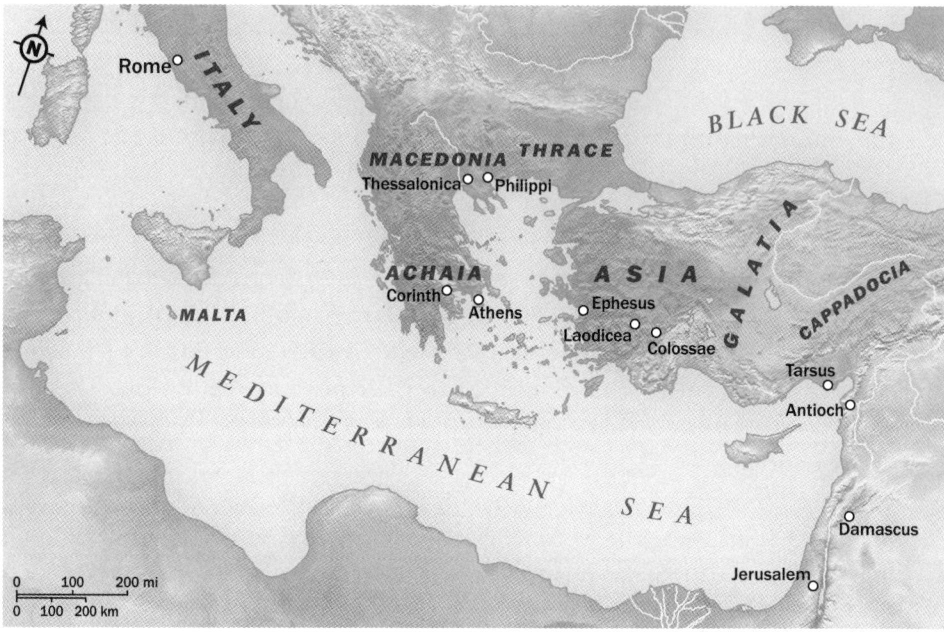

Even Paul's greeting to his readers is noteworthy. By using the words *grace* and *peace*, Paul reiterates that this letter was written for both Jews and Gentiles in the church. (For more information on this, reread the introduction to Colossians on page 111.)

DAY 2

Colossians 1:3–5a

READ COLOSSIANS 1:3–5A

Paul's affection for the Colossians and the good report he'd received about their faith were immediately apparent in his letter.

Review 1:3.

1. Who did Paul thank when he prayed for the Colossians? Why is this noteworthy?

Some translations essentially say, "*We continually pray for you.*" But this is more accurately translated as "We always thank God . . . when we pray for you." In other words, every time Paul and his companions prayed for the Colossians, they were filled with thanksgiving about them. And Paul knew that God was the author of their faith and love—they didn't muster it on their own.

Yesterday, we touched on the theme of Paul's letter, subtly presented in the first two verses. Here, he doubled down on this treatise when he referred to Jesus as "the Lord Jesus Christ." In this single statement, he proclaimed Jesus as fully divine (Lord), fully man (Jesus), and the Messiah (Christ).[1] As you continue through this study, keep an eye out for the number of times you see the word *Christ*.

Review 1:4.

2. What two things about them was he thankful for?

Remember, Paul had never met the Colossians. But despite that, he was already well aware of the bond of unity among them.

★ 3. How does it encourage you to know that, right now, all over the world, there are individuals, groups, and churches worshiping Jesus and anticipating His return? In what ways do you feel connected to believers you've never met?

Review 1:5a.

In the two and a half verses we're studying today, Paul tied a cord of three strands, describing the hallmark of a growing Christian.

★ 4. Can you identify the three words that make up the cord? (See 1 Corinthians 13:13 for help.) Write them on the three strands below. How do these three elements, when tied together, create unity among believers?

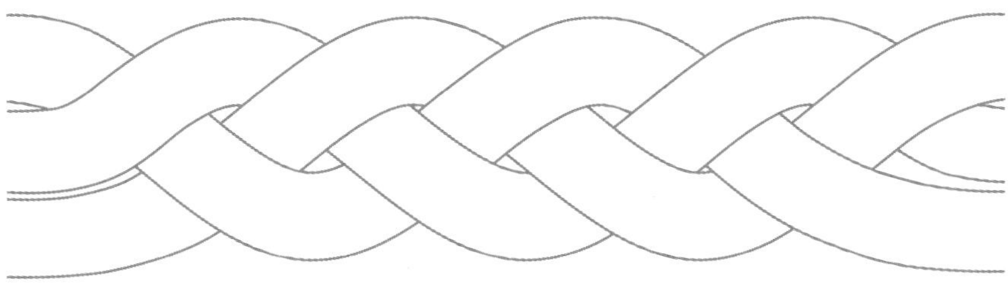

Life wasn't easy for those who were building the early church. But their hope—their "confident expectation"[2]—was that Christ was preparing a place for them (John 14:3). Today, we live with that same confidence! The promise of heaven empowers us to be people who are bold in our faith, generous with our love, and patient in our hope. Paul called out and praised these traits of the Colossians' because he knew that no matter what they faced, the kingdom awaited them.

DAY 3

Colossians 1:5b–8

READ COLOSSIANS 1:5B–8

Review 1:5b.

1. What was Paul referring to that they had already heard about? (Hint: See 1:5a.)

The Colossians had heard of this promise when Epaphras shared the gospel with them. Paul used the word *truth* and the word *gospel* interchangeably here. He essentially said, *"The word of truth—that is, the gospel."* The Colossians, as well as other churches in the region, were being challenged with false teaching. As he continued writing, Paul clearly identified the heresies and taught the Colossians the best way to identify a lie: by knowing the truth.

Review 1:6.

2. The gospel had not reached only the Colossians. Where else had it traveled? And what was it doing?

This wasn't growth by addition—it was growth by multiplication. The news of Jesus's death, burial, and resurrection was spreading like wildfire throughout the entire Roman Empire. Even now, the message of the gospel will not be stopped until Jesus returns. Once people hear, understand, and accept the truth, the natural response is to share it with others!

The word *understood* here is *epiginōskō*, and it means "to know thoroughly" and "to recognize a thing to be what it really is." Some refer to this as the truth "moving from your head to your heart."

★ 3. Think about your own experience. Was there a time gap between when you first heard the truth and when you understood and received it? Or did you immediately understand and receive it, like the Colossians did? Explain. (Neither answer is the "right" answer; both answers are good and beautiful.)

When the Colossians recognized God's grace for what it really was—God's unmerited favor toward them—it was a turning point in their lives. The Colossians not only *heard* it. *They got it.*

Review 1:7.

Hearing and understanding was a turning point in Epaphras's life too. As soon as he grabbed hold of this, he returned to his countrymen and shared the good news with them. And it appears that he not only shared the gospel with them but stayed to invest in their spiritual growth. All we know about Epaphras is that he served the Lord faithfully. May the same be said of us.

Review 1:8.

Because of Epaphras's eternal investment in Colossae, they were a growing body of believers—not necessarily in size, though that's likely too. They were growing in *love for one another.*

This verse is the only place in the entire letter to the Colossians where the Holy Spirit is mentioned—and it's in reference to their love for one another. There's a lot we don't know or understand about the Holy Spirit. But we know His work when we see it. And love for one another is one of His trademarks.

It's clear that the church at Colossae took Jesus's words to heart.

4. Read John 13:35 and fill in the blanks.

"By this all people will know that you are my disciples, if you have ____________

for ____________ ________________________."

DAY 4

Colossians 1:9–10

READ COLOSSIANS 1:9–10

Review 1:9a.

Paul was encouraged by what he'd learned about the Colossians. But the news of their faithfulness also motivated him to intense prayer.

1. Look back at 1:3–8. What five things had Paul heard about the church in Colossae?

A.

B.

C.

D.

E.

The church in Colossae had an excellent reputation, but as we learned from Paul's letter to the Philippians, this was no reason for them to take their foot off the gas. It was all the more important for them to recognize that they had not already obtained perfection (see Philippians 3:12).

With a heartfelt desire that they continue growing, Paul spent the next four verses sharing the specific ways he diligently prayed for them.

★ 2. Is there someone who prays for you diligently and consistently? If so, write a prayer below thanking God for their selfless intercession. If not, consider asking someone to be a prayer partner with you, using 1:9–12 as a guide.

Review 1:9b.

The word for *wisdom* here is *sophia*, and it's the root of our English words *sophistication* and *philosophy*.[1] We know from Greco-Roman history that knowledge and philosophy were held in high esteem. As we'll see later, this type of human "wisdom" even began to encroach upon the church, which is why Paul was intentional to insert the adjective *spiritual* here. He didn't want the Colossians to grow in worldly wisdom; he wanted them to grow in wisdom that came from the fear of the Lord (Proverbs 9:10) and in understanding from the Holy Spirit.

Review 1:10.

Growing in spiritual wisdom and understanding isn't just getting wiser for wisdom's sake, and it's certainly not for puffing ourselves up.

★ 3. How did Paul say growing in wisdom would change the way they walked? And what two things would be the result? Have you found this to be true in your own life? Explain.

The fruit of wisdom is obedience. In fact, when we don't seek the wisdom and guidance of the Holy Spirit, our efforts to grow in knowledge are empty and prideful. As one pastor wrote, "How much can you do without Him? Nothing! So what is everything you do without Him? Nothing!"[2]

But the concept of bearing fruit through the power of Christ was not a novel idea. Another Teacher had shared this truth some three decades before Paul ever penned this letter.

4. According to John 15:5–8, how do we bear fruit? And how much fruit will we bear if we follow these instructions?

Paul, a man with more knowledge than most preachers of his day, could bear witness to Jesus's words: "Apart from me, you can do nothing" (John 15:5).

DAY 5

Colossians 1:11–14

READ COLOSSIANS 1:11–14

Looking back at 1:10, it can feel like Paul put a lot of pressure on the Colossians—and us, for that matter. This is weighty.

They're supposed to "walk in a manner *worthy of the Lord*" and be "*fully pleasing* to Him," "bearing fruit in *every* good work" all while "*increasing* in the knowledge of God"?*

How in the world can we measure up to this standard?

The answer is we can't—not in our own strength. Fortunately, nobody is asking us to.

Review 1:11–12.

1. Where did Paul tell the Colossians to find their strength?

A. In pulling themselves up by their bootstraps

B. In the gym

C. In living a perfect, sin-free life

D. In God's glorious might

E. In the perfect combination of God's grace and their own mental toughness

Without God's power working in and through us, life can start to feel like we're spinning lots of very large, very fragile plates. But God's strength empowers us to patiently endure with *joy* and *thanksgiving*!

This news must've felt like an exhale for the believers in Colossae. Yes, God had put a high calling on their lives, but He wouldn't leave them

* Emphasis added to the Scripture quotes in this paragraph.

alone to accomplish the work. The Colossians were granted the hope of heaven (1:5)—simply because their heavenly Father had qualified them. They didn't have to earn it.

Review 1:13–14.

This passage features a concept that many refer to as the Great Exchange. Every believer—from the Colossians to the person sitting next to you at Bible study—was born into the domain of darkness. We were far from God, lost in this fallen world.

But God plucked us out of darkness and transferred us to His kingdom. The kingdom of light. The kingdom of His beloved Son, Jesus.

★ 2. **Look up the definition of *redemption*.** Then, in your own words, write a description of the Great Exchange below.

If you belong to Christ, you've been delivered once and for all. Your hope is secure. Indeed, *He does the doing*. But let's not breeze past this.

3. According to today's passage, what five things does God do for us?

A.

B.

C.

D.

E.

★ 4. Which of these things is most encouraging to you in your current season of life?

End your day with this prayer: *Heavenly Father, I know I've fallen short of Your standard of perfection, but because of the finished work of Your Son, Jesus, You have qualified me for eternal life in Your kingdom! You have delivered me, redeemed me, and strengthened me. Even when I may not feel it, I know I can rejoice in the beautiful inheritance granted to me through Your Son—because He's where the joy is!*

5. What stood out to you most in this week's study? Why?

6. What did you learn or relearn about God and His character this week?

DAY 6

Corresponding Psalm & Prayer

READ PSALM 33

1. What correlation do you see between Psalm 33 and this week's study?

2. What portions of this psalm stand out to you most?

3. Close by praying this prayer aloud:

Father,

Your Word is upright, and we trust in Your holy name. All Your work is done in faithfulness; You are our help and our shield. You love righteousness and justice, and You have made us saints. The whole earth is full of Your steadfast love, and You've given us grace upon grace. We stand in awe of You, and it is right that we praise You!

You've given me faith, and I repent of all the times I've doubted Your plans. You've given me hope, and I repent of all the times I've put my hope in things that fade away. You've given me love, and I repent of all the times I've treated others with hatred, disdain, and indifference.

Will You once again move Your truth from my head to my heart? I want to understand the beauty of Your unmerited favor—to really and truly get it. Like the Colossians, may I be the kind of person who causes others to thank God when they pray for me. May they see my love for all Your saints. As I abide in You, strengthened according to Your glorious might, may I increase in the knowledge and understanding of You, and may I bear fruit.

Apart from You, I can do nothing, so I surrender my life to You, Lord—every moment of my day, each decision I make, I yield my will and way to Your perfect will and way.

I love You too. Amen.

DAY 7

Rest, Catch Up, or Dig Deeper

WEEKLY CHALLENGE

Even though Paul had never visited Colossae, their church had a reputation of love and faithfulness. This week, seize the opportunity to increase the beauty of the reputation your local church has in your community. Invite someone to join you at church—someone who doesn't have a church of their own or who wouldn't consider themselves a Christian. Seek every opportunity to make them feel welcomed and loved!

WEEK 7

Colossians 1:15–29

Scripture to Memorize

For by him all things were created, in heaven and on earth, visible and invisible, whether thrones or dominions or rulers or authorities—all things were created through him and for him.

Colossians 1:16

DAILY BIBLE READING

Day 1: Colossians 1:15–17
Day 2: Colossians 1:18–20
Day 3: Colossians 1:21–23
Day 4: Colossians 1:24–27
Day 5: Colossians 1:28–29
Day 6: Psalm 89
Day 7: Catch-Up Day

Corresponds to Day 349 of *The Bible Recap.*

WEEKLY CHALLENGE

See page 149 for more information.

DAY 1

Colossians 1:15–17

READ COLOSSIANS 1:15–17

Review 1:15.

Most scholars agree that 1:15–20 is an early church poem. Some think it might have been a hymn, perhaps sung during worship.[1] Either way the content and language within this section were meant to be concise, powerful, and easy to remember in order to dispel some of the heretical teaching threatening the Colossian church. (For more information, reread the introduction to Colossians on page 111.)

One of the popular heresies claimed that Jesus was simply one of God's creations and therefore wasn't God. Paul's first two declarations about Christ set out to dismantle this false and dangerous way of thinking.

1. Begin filling in the table below with Paul's statements about Christ (the first one has been done for you). **Using a Bible dictionary or Greek lexicon, look up *firstborn* (1:15) and write the definition.** Leave the third column blank for now. (You'll complete half of this table today and the second half on Day 2.)

WHO IS JESUS?

Verse	Definition	In your own words
He is the . . . image of the invisible God (1:15)	*Image: visible representation, something expressing the exact likeness of (God), likeness, or representation.*	*Jesus is God, the exact representation of the invisible God to humanity.*
He is the firstborn . . . ___ ___ ______ (1:15)	Firstborn:	Jesus is
By Him all things . . . ____ ______ (1:16)		Jesus is
All things were created . . . ______ ___ ___ ___ ___ (1:16)		Jesus is the goal of all creation. He is the reason for all creation.
He is . . . ______ ___ ______ (1:17)	Before:	Jesus is
In Him all things . . . ____ ______ (1:17)		Jesus is
He is . . . ___ ____ ___ ___ ____ (1:18)	Head:	Jesus is
He is the beginning . . . ___ ______ ____ ___ ____ (1:18)	Beginning: active cause, origin, first thing in a series, leader	Jesus is
He is preeminent (1:18)	Preeminent:	Jesus is
In Him all the . . . ______ ___ ___ ___ _____ ___ ______ (1:19)	Dwell: to settle down in a place, to live	Jesus is
Through Him to reconcile . . . ___ ______ ___ _____(1:20)	Reconciliation:	Jesus is
He made peace by ___ _____ ___ ___ _____ (1:20)		Jesus is

The phrase "firstborn of all creation" may seem confusing at first, and unfortunately this has led some people to wrongly believe that Jesus was created. *Not true!* He can't be a created being—Jesus is God Himself (John 1:18). Jesus is the Father's exact likeness, and He represented God's will and character on earth. As you continue this study, you'll find out more about why Scripture says it isn't possible for Jesus to be a created being.

Here, Paul was expressing the priority of Christ by calling Him the firstborn. In ancient cultures, the firstborn was the one who received the inheritance. Some translations render this "the firstborn *over* all creation" (emphasis added), which can help more clearly express the truth of Christ's superiority. He is *over* it all, and He is the rightful *heir* of it all!

★ 2. Referencing 1:15, fill in the first empty cell of the third column in the table above. In your own words, use Paul's statement to explain who Jesus is.

Review 1:16.

3. Complete column 1 for 1:16.

This verse helps further debunk any claims that Christ might be a created being. Not only was He not created, but *He* is the one who created everything! Paul emphasized the scope of "all things" including heaven and earth—everything seen and unseen.

There are four additional created things mentioned in this verse: thrones, dominions, rulers, and authorities. Some scholars think this list refers to only angelic ranks (including fallen and unfallen angels) and may have had to do with the false teaching in Colossae. Others believe this could refer to both angelic beings and humans.[2] Regardless, Paul's point was clear: Jesus created everything, and all creation exists in reference to Him.

4. Complete column 3 for 1:16.

Review 1:17.

5. Complete columns 1–2 for 1:17.

This verse helps us understand Christ's relationship to His creation. He is eternal, existing before all created things. He has authority over all creation. And finally, He is the one who sustains creation.

6. Complete column 3 for 1:17.

That was a lot of information, so let's zoom out. In this small section, Paul was providing the Colossians and us an opportunity to marvel at the reality of Christ. *He is God*. He is the Creator *and* the Sustainer. Everything—seen and unseen—exists in relation to Him.

★ 7. In your own words, summarize what today's passage reveals about Christ and His creation.

DAY 2

Colossians 1:18–20

READ COLOSSIANS 1:18–20

Paul began this poem focused on the truth that Christ is God, the creator of all things. Here, Paul wrote about Christ's relationship to His *new* creation—the church.

Review 1:18.

1. In the table from Day 1, complete columns 1–2 for 1:18. **Use a Bible dictionary or Greek lexicon to look up the definitions.**

Christ is the *authority* over His body (the church). He is also the *origin* and *initiator* of His people. Through His resurrection, Jesus established a present and a future reality that bring great hope. The present reality: You are a new creation the moment you come to know Christ. The future reality: You will be made new and fully like Christ when all are raised from the dead at His return (1 John 3:2; 1 Corinthians 15:49).

★ 2. Complete column 3 for 1:18.

Review 1:19.

3. Complete column 1 for 1:19.

The final two verses of this poem speak to the incredible truth of salvation. Although we know Christ was both fully God and fully man, Paul highlighted the "fullness of God" here to combat the false teaching in Colossae that claimed Christ was less than God. (Note: This is so important you'll see it again in 2:9.) Paul emphasized that in Jesus the complete reality of God dwelled. And only through Jesus is reconciliation possible.

4. Complete column 3 for 1:19.

Review 1:20.

5. Complete columns 1–2 for 1:20.

This is the fulfillment of Isaiah 53:5, which reads, "Upon him was the chastisement that brought us peace." Through Christ's sacrifice—a willing offering of Himself on the cross—humanity could be reconciled to God. This reconciliation wasn't just for humanity; it involved restoring all things to their rightly ordered relationship to Christ.

Paul bookended the poem by reorienting creation—whether on earth or in heaven—to its source and Savior, Jesus Christ. This reality was secured on the cross; and although we see glimmers of the reconciliation of all things, the fullness won't be realized until Jesus returns.

Did you notice the active agent in this verse? This desperate predicament of sin and separation from God—it could only be solved by God Himself. *He does the doing!*

★ 6. Complete column 3 for 1:20.

That was a theologically dense section of Scripture. Hopefully you were encouraged by the beauty and truth of who Christ is as our leader, reconciler, and peacemaker!

DAY 3

Colossians 1:21–23

READ COLOSSIANS 1:21–23

On Days 1 and 2, you wrote down twelve affirmations about Jesus. Keep these in mind as we continue studying this letter. Paul thought it was essential to proclaim these truths before reminding or teaching the Colossians anything else.

Review 1:21.

Paul brought the reality of 1:15–20 directly to the Colossians—they were in desperate need of the reconciliation and peace only Jesus could provide.

1. What was the Colossians' past state? Circle all that apply.

   A. Alienated
   B. Hostile in mind
   C. Doing evil deeds
   D. Healthy and happy
   E. Blissful

Review 1:22.

Once again Paul referenced Christ's death as the only way for reconciliation to take place. Paul mentioned "his body of flesh," directly opposing another false teaching that glorified the spiritual above the material. Christ lived in a human body and His death occurred in this same body; and only through that sacrificial death were the Colossians able to experience peace and unity with God.

2. Highlight the pronouns in the phrases below. Then answer the question.

HE has NOW reconciled

By HIS death

In His BODY OF flesh

To present YOU before HIM

Who makes this reality possible?

3. How did Paul describe the Colossians' present state of reconciliation?

Review 1:23.

Paul knew the Colossians were faithful (1:2, 4). He encouraged them to continue in this same way: remaining established and settled in their faith in Christ. This was all the more necessary given the shaky ground presented by the false teachers. However, with the Colossians' faith and hope firmly planted in the good news of Jesus, nothing would be able to move them.

★ 4. What truths have you learned in this study that help you remain "stable and steadfast" in your faith? Explain.

The word translated *minister* (*diakonos*) can also mean "servant," "attendant," and even "waiter." Paul first referred to himself as an apostle (1:1), yet he also understood that part of being a messenger of Christ meant being a servant.

DAY 4

Colossians 1:24–27

READ COLOSSIANS 1:24–27

Review 1:24.

1. Fill in the blanks below.

"Now I ______________ in my ________________ for __________ sake."

Paul often rejoiced in the midst of sufferings (Romans 5:3; Philippians 1:18–19). And here, he seemed to connect this suffering with the Colossians themselves. It was *for their sake*. Most scholars agree that "filling up what is lacking in Christ's afflictions" is the most challenging phrase to interpret in this epistle.[1] To avoid confusion, we'll cover what this doesn't mean first.

Christ's death on the cross was sufficient and dealt once for all with the problem of sin and separation from God. Therefore, this *doesn't* mean there is anything lacking in Christ's death or His suffering on the cross. It's helpful to note the word translated *afflictions* (*thlipsis*) is not the word used to describe Christ's suffering on the cross.[2]

Here are two ways we can think about this phrase.

Option 1	Option 2
It's clear throughout Scripture that all Christians will suffer, and this is understood as "suffering with Christ" (see Romans 8:17). Paul considered himself to be participating in Christ's afflictions on behalf of the Colossians and the church.	This refers to Christ suffering with Paul, because the Spirit of God indwelt Paul. In essence, Christ suffers when His body (the church) experiences affliction or persecution. Paul seemed also to "suffer with" or on "behalf of" Christ's church.

★ 2. **Look up 1:24 in the NLT and Amplified Bible.** Based on these translations and what you've learned so far, which option makes more sense to you? Explain.

Review 1:25–27.

Paul had been given a great responsibility from God to proclaim this message (see Acts 9:1–19), and he participated in the work joyfully, despite suffering.

3. Using 1:26–27 as your guide, answer the questions below.

How long was the mystery hidden?

When was it revealed?

Who did God reveal the mystery to?

What is the mystery (reference Ephesians 3:6 for additional help)?

The scope of God's glorious plan was lavish and abundant. The family of God was growing, and against all odds, the Gentiles were equal members in the body of Christ. Commentary writer Dr. Thomas Constable wrote, "That God would save Gentiles was no new revelation (e.g., Isa. 49:6), but that He would dwell in them and deal with them on the same basis as He did Jews was new revelation."[3] This was the "hope of glory" for the Gentiles, and us too.

DAY 5

Colossians 1:28–29

READ COLOSSIANS 1:28–29

Review 1:28.

1. Fill in the graphic below.

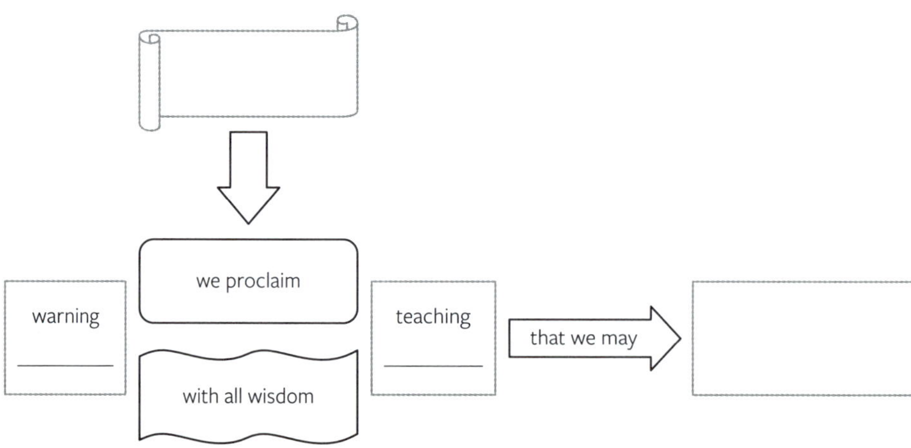

"Him we proclaim" might sound a little strange in English. However, the translators kept this word order on purpose, keeping the most important word at the beginning of the sentence for emphasis—*Him*.

Paul moved from discussing his ministry of proclamation and here included those with him in Rome and the Colossians too ("we"). The body of Christ, His church, has always had one main mission—to preach Christ to everyone.

2. **Look up *warning* (1:28) in a Greek lexicon and write the definition below.**

★ 3. How have you seen the combination of warning and teaching lead to greater maturity in your life? Name a few of the people who helped you.

Review 1:29.

Paul's goal in ministry was gospel proclamation, which resulted in mature believers and healthy churches. And this work was difficult. Paul's labor was often burdensome—leading to sleepless nights and exhaustion (2 Corinthians 11:27–28). Yet Paul knew that the end goal was worth it. He also knew there was a greater power at work within him.

The energy of Christ was what compelled, strengthened, and empowered Paul. This verse beautifully represents the mysterious tension between God's sovereignty and human responsibility. Paul was not lazy, banking on the grace of Christ to "pick up the slack" for him. Nor was Paul overly anxious or concerned that everything rested on his shoulders. Instead, he labored on with the supernatural power and energy of Christ.

★ 4. Highlight or circle any similar words or phrases in the passages below.

Colossians 1:29	1 Corinthians 15:10	Ephesians 3:20 NIV
"For this I toil, struggling with all his energy that he powerfully works within me."	"But by the grace of God I am what I am, and his grace toward me was not in vain. On the contrary, I worked harder than any of them, though it was not I, but the grace of God that is with me."	"Now to him who is able to do immeasurably more than all we ask or imagine, according to his power that is at work within us . . ."

How do these passages inform or challenge your view of God's sovereignty and your own responsibility?

Look back to the table you completed on Days 1 and 2. Christ, God Himself—the creator and sustainer of all things—is the same Christ whose power is at work in you! His energy is your energy. His strength is your strength. Him we proclaim, because He's where the joy is!

5. What stood out to you most in this week's study? Why?

6. What did you learn or relearn about God and His character this week?

DAY 6

Corresponding Psalm & Prayer

READ PSALM 89

1. What correlation do you see between Psalm 89 and this week's study?

2. What portions of this psalm stand out to you most?

3. Close by praying this prayer aloud:

Father,

You sent Your firstborn—the visible image of the invisible God. Since before the beginning, He has always been. Jesus, You are God.

Spirit, You are God. Father, You are God. It is You we proclaim—the triune God of the universe! I will sing of You forever: Your righteousness, Your justice, Your faithfulness, Your steadfast love.

Father, You are our supreme authority, but I've insisted on my own way. Jesus, You are our example, but I've lived how I've seen fit. Spirit, You guide us into truth, but I've chased after lies. Lord, I turn from my sins, and I turn back to You.

Help me live every moment with deep reassurance of this truth: You live in me! Help me live every moment with an unwavering urgency: I want to proclaim You! I want to make Your faithfulness known to all generations. I want to continue in the faith, stable and steadfast, never shifting from the hope of the gospel.

As I depend on Your energy to sustain me, I surrender my life to You, Lord—every moment of my day, each decision I make, I yield my will and way to Your perfect will and way.

I love You too. Amen.

DAY 7

Rest, Catch Up, or Dig Deeper

WEEKLY CHALLENGE

On Days 1 and 2, you wrote twelve statements affirming the truth of who Christ is. Get creative and use your favorite supplies or skills to turn your list into a piece of art.

WEEK 8

Colossians 2

Scripture to Memorize

And he is before all things, and in him all things hold together.

Colossians 1:17

DAILY BIBLE READING

Day 1: Colossians 2:1–5

Day 2: Colossians 2:6–7

Day 3: Colossians 2:8–15

Day 4: Colossians 2:16–19

Day 5: Colossians 2:20–23

Day 6: Psalm 103

Day 7: Catch-Up Day

Corresponds to Day 349 of *The Bible Recap.*

WEEKLY CHALLENGE

See page 170 for more information.

DAY 1

Colossians 2:1–5

READ COLOSSIANS 2:1–5

Review 2:1.

1. Circle Laodicea on the map from our study of Colossians 1 (see page 116).

Although Paul hadn't met the Colossians, or the Laodiceans, he still cared deeply for them. Early Christian communities were closely connected, and Paul described his concern for them with the word *struggle*, suggesting intense effort or even agony.

Review 2:2–3.

As Enduring Word's commentary says, discouraged hearts are easy prey for the enemy.[1] And Paul wanted the Colossians to avoid falling prey.

2. What three goals did Paul have for the Colossians, as shown by his use of the word *that*?

The word *encouraged* (*parakaleō*) implied comfort, exhortation, and strength. Paul's desire for them to be "knit together" showed his longing for unity, and love was the glue that made unity possible. It led them to enjoy true riches.

But Paul wasn't referring to literal riches; he was showing the immense value of knowing the truths of Jesus. He emphasized that through encouragement, unity, and love, believers could be confident they fully understood the gospel and certain they knew the truth. Nothing was missing and nothing needed to be added.

This assurance wasn't superficial. It was deeply rooted in their community's collective understanding of who Jesus is. The Colossians and the Laodiceans knew the gospel.

★ 3. Look back at Week 1 of this study. In brief, what is the gospel?

"God's mystery" referred to the previously hidden answers to these questions: Who was the Messiah? When would He come? What would He do?

What was once unknown had been made clear through Christ! The "mystery" wasn't a mystery at all. Whenever a believer comes to know Christ, they have immediate access to all the treasures found in Him.

Knowledge, in this instance, describes one's understanding of truth—a.k.a., the gospel. Wisdom is the practical application of knowledge. It describes a person's ability to make godly decisions in their daily life. Paul emphasized that true wisdom wasn't found in the secretive teachings or philosophies that were circulating at the time.

Review 2:4.

Paul wasn't saying that the Colossians had been deceived. He was aware false teachings were spreading, and he wanted to make sure they knew that even though those teachings might have sounded convincing, they were wrong. Anything that distorts the gospel—or adds to it—is *not the gospel at all.*

Review 2:5.

Though Paul hadn't met the Colossians in person, distance didn't diminish his care or their unity in Christ. Paul rejoiced because he'd heard the Colossians were on the right track—they weren't being deceived by the distorted teachings. "Good order" points to a disciplined, well-organized community—a church committed to godly living and to the true gospel. Paul praised their unwavering faith as a key to resisting deception.

4. Who in your life shows unwavering faith in Christ? Write their initials below and send them a quick note or text to encourage them.

DAY 2

Colossians 2:6–7

READ COLOSSIANS 2:6–7

In today's reading, Paul emphasized a key theme of his letter: union with Christ. Believers are spiritually joined to Jesus in His death, resurrection, and exaltation—and this reality is the foundation for our salvation and daily walk. Grasping this truth is essential, because union with Christ not only shapes our identity but transforms the way we live.

1. To highlight this theme, we'll briefly jump to tomorrow's verses, then return to today's. Match each phrase with its reference.

"walk in him"	2:13
"built up in him"	2:11
"for in him"	2:10
"you have been filled in him"	2:6
"In him also you"	2:9
"buried with him in baptism"	2:6
"made alive together with him"	2:12

Review 2:6.

★ 2. Paul used the word *therefore* at the start of today's text, so we must ask, What's the *therefore* there for? Summarize yesterday's reading in your own words.

The word *received* wasn't just about gaining knowledge—it meant embracing a person: Christ Jesus as Lord. Embracing Jesus involves acknowledging His authority and submitting to Him. It isn't merely acknowledging that He exists or even that He is God—after all, the demons know and believe that (James 2:19). Believing in Jesus through faith involves a change of heart that prompts us to live differently in response to who He is and what He's done.

3. Look at our study of 1:3. What stance did Paul take when he called Jesus "our Lord Jesus Christ"?

He's taking the same stance here in 2:6. It's like Paul was saying, *"In response to who Jesus is, live differently."* The Greek verb for *walk* (*peripateō*) implies ongoing, daily conduct. Paul was urging believers to align their lives with Christ continually. Their relationship with Jesus was meant to shape every part of life—that's union with Christ in action!

★ 4. Is your faith in Jesus infiltrating all areas of your life? Are there any areas you don't want Jesus to change? Explain.

Review 2:7.

Just as tree roots grow deep to help a tree stand firm against the wind, Paul wanted the Colossians to be rooted in their union with Christ so they could keep growing and not be swayed by the world. *To be established* means "to be strengthened and made secure." Paul urged them to cling to the truth they'd already been taught—they didn't need anything else. If their roots were strong, they would be too.

5. Finish drawing the tree. What fundamental truths do the roots represent? Write them beside the roots. (Hint: The roots reflect what God has done. Use today's definition of "union with Christ" and your gospel summary from yesterday for help.) Tomorrow we'll elaborate on what could have tempted the Colossians to be swayed.

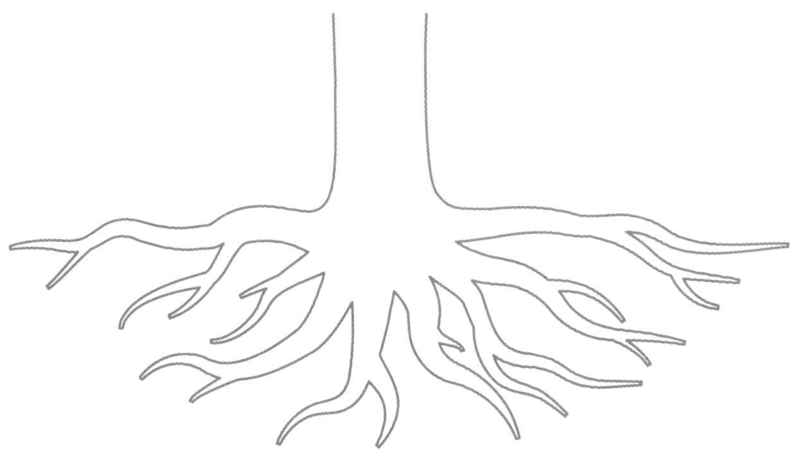

When believers realize that the foundation of our faith is built on God's work—not ours—our natural response should be gratitude. Paul described thanksgiving as an ongoing, overflowing reaction to God's grace—and we'll see that it's a theme in this letter (and in Paul's other letters as well). Have you thanked Him today?

DAY 3

Colossians 2:8–15

READ COLOSSIANS 2:8–15

Paul wanted the Colossians to recognize opposition, then cling to truth in response. A popular belief system, later called Gnosticism, included the teaching that secret knowledge (*gnosis*) was the key to salvation. These false teachers denied Jesus's full humanity and believed the spiritual world was more important than physical realities on earth. Paul disagreed. *To live is Christ, right?*

Review 2:8.

The phrase "takes you captive" implied being carried off like plunder. Paul warned that false teachers weren't just wrong—they were predators, "spiritual kidnappers."[1] Paul was likely suggesting that gnostic teaching was tied to demonic influences (i.e., "elemental spirits").

But how was Paul so sure? *If spiritual teaching isn't rooted in the gospel or if it adds something to the gospel, it's not only empty—it's dangerous.*

★ 1. What are some popular philosophies modern Christians encounter or could fall prey to if they aren't rooted in Christ? List these potentially tempting ideologies beside the tree you drew yesterday.

Review 2:9–10.

2. Based on your knowledge of Gnosticism so far, why do you think Paul specifically emphasized that the "fullness of deity dwells bodily" in Christ?

★ 3. Fill in the table below.

Summarize Colossians 1:15–20	
Write out Colossians 2:9	
How does 1:15–20 help you better understand 2:9?	

Paul opposed the gnostic idea that believers needed to be pursuing "extra" revelation. Because the Colossians were believers, they'd been filled with the Spirit and therefore had everything they needed for life and godliness (2 Peter 1:3).

Review 2:11–12.

4. Look back at our study of Philippians 3. What did we learn about circumcision?

Paul emphasized that salvation is entirely God's work—it's not something earned through external acts, such as circumcision. The phrase "putting off the body of the flesh" included the Greek word *apekdysis*, meaning "a complete removal"—like shedding dirty, sweaty clothes and then desiring to put on something clean immediately.

The "circumcision of Christ" probably referred to the spiritual cutting away of our sinful standing before God (which marked us prior to salvation). Through our union with Christ, we're joined to His death, and Paul used baptism to illustrate this. Baptism is an outward sign of an inward change. It doesn't save, but faith in God's resurrection power certainly does.

5. How many times did Paul use the words *you* and *your* in today's reading (2:8–15)?

Review 2:13–15.

Paul reminded the Colossians that their identity was in Christ—not in their culture or ethnic background. Apart from Jesus they were dead in sin (Romans 3:23). In Paul's day, the "record of debt" was an actual Roman ledger; those who missed a payment owed interest as penalty. In a similar way, Christ's death paid our sin debt—which we accrued by falling short of God's law (Romans 3:20). Therefore, believers no longer stand condemned, and Satan's forces have been defeated (Romans 8:1; 1 Corinthians 15:55–57). Through faith, full forgiveness and resurrection life are instantly applied.

In Christ, there's no probation period—just complete pardon.

DAY 4

Colossians 2:16–19

READ COLOSSIANS 2:16–19

Review 2:16–18.

Paul rejected any attempts to earn favor with God through religious rule-keeping. He wasn't suggesting that believers should "do their own thing," or "refuse to let anyone judge them." Paul was essentially saying, "*Don't be bound by legalism.*" The term *legalism* often describes any attempt to earn favor with God through religious rule-keeping.

★ 1. Have you ever been inclined to believe that God would love you more or give you what you wanted if you practiced more spiritual disciplines (reading your Bible, going to church, fasting, sharing the gospel, etc.)? Explain.

During the Colossians' time, asceticism was a common belief system that had its fair share of flaws and dangers (Paul later calls it worthless in 2:23). The ascetics believed in mutilating the flesh as an act of worship or spiritual maturity, as well as "abstinence [in marriage] . . . and extreme self-denial."[1] The false teachers likely advocated for harsh discipline of the body as a way for people to achieve religious superiority.

"Food and drink" likely referred to dietary restrictions found in Jewish law (Leviticus 11) or ascetic practices tied to false teachers. Paul's point wasn't that food laws, Jewish festivals, or keeping the Sabbath were evil, but that the rules surrounding these things were no longer binding. When Jesus fulfilled the laws of the Old Testament (Matthew 5:17), He relieved His followers of the *burden* of keeping it. Instead, they were free to abide by the law for their own delight, not out of fear.

Here, Paul wasn't necessarily suggesting one throw out the festivals in their entirety. In another letter, he basically said, *"You can keep them—but make sure you're first and foremost celebrating the right thing: Christ's finished work"* (see 1 Corinthians 5:8). Paul didn't want the Colossians to replace the reality of Christ's finished work with the rituals of Jewish celebrations.

2. Look back at your study of 1:16. What did Christ create?

It's likely that the false teachers wrongly exalted angels as a pathway to spiritual maturity, and they claimed superiority based on mystical experiences. The authority of the false teachers seemed to come from personal experiences apart from the already revealed truth of Jesus. They boasted in prideful, self-generated revelations.

Review 2:19.

★ 3. Look back at your study of 1:18. What does it mean for Christ to be head of the church?

The whole body of Christ, the church, isn't a physical building—it's the people of God! And Christ is the source of life, unity, and growth for everyone in His church. Paul's main accusation against the false teachers was that they'd abandoned Christ, who is the head of His church. True spiritual growth occurs through union with Christ and His church, not through man-made religious systems or mystical experiences.

The phrase "nourished and knit" suggests imagery of a living, functioning body that grows organically rather than through mechanical rule-keeping. Growth can come only from God. *He does the doing.* Man-made spirituality doesn't produce legitimate spiritual maturity—only God does, through Christ.

DAY 5

Colossians 2:20–23

READ COLOSSIANS 2:20–23

Review 2:20.

★ 1. Based on our study of 2:6–7, what is union with Christ?

2. Based on our study of 2:8, what were the elemental spirits?

Union with Christ severs the believer from legalistic requirements and systems of self-righteousness. Paul was adamant: If the Colossians had died with Christ, why would they ever want to act like they were still under worldly bondage?

Review 2:21.

Paul gave an example of what living under worldly bondage could have looked like for the Colossians. If they'd given in to the false teachers, they would have followed three specific ascetic commands.

3. Which of the following is *not* one of the ascetic commands?

   A. Do not handle

   B. Do not taste

   C. Do not laugh

   D. Do not touch

These rules were harsh, external, and lifeless. They focused on prioritizing outward acts while neglecting inner transformation. The order in which Paul listed the commands may have implied increasing levels of strictness. Nonetheless, we can be certain that Paul wasn't a fan of these rules.

Review 2:22.

Paul made it clear just how ineffective he found the ascetic rules to be by comparing them to "things that . . . perish." Think about what happens to bread that's left in the back of a cupboard for too long—it gets moldy and is no longer edible. It's useless! Paul argued that these ascetic restrictions were temporary and material. They weren't eternal and they didn't lead to lasting spiritual impact. Said differently, they weren't in line with the way and power of Christ.

The ascetic teachings were made up by men—they weren't God's idea. Extra rules or religious acts are powerless to change hearts and attain perfection. Paul knew lasting lifestyle change stemmed from loving Jesus and understanding what He did on our behalf. One's love for Jesus *should* lead to behavior change, but behavior modification isn't where spiritual transformation starts.

4. Match each verse reference with the summary of its contents.

Isaiah 29:13	People draw near to God with their words but wrongly honor God with lip service and rote tradition.
Mark 7:7	People worship in vain and teach man's ideologies as if they were God's.

Review 2:23.

The Colossians could have been tempted to think that legalism, mysticism, and asceticism were wise practices or "more spiritual" lifestyles, because these were deceptive teachings. Paul called them "self-made," which meant they were made up by humans—they were worthless ideologies. External religion can't transform hearts or successfully combat sin. Paul wanted to make sure the Colossians knew they didn't need anything apart from Christ. True victory over the indulgences of the flesh (sin) is found only through union with Christ. He's where the joy is!

★ 5. What stood out to you most in this week's study? Why?

6. What did you learn or relearn about God and His character this week?

DAY 6

Corresponding Psalm & Prayer

READ PSALM 103

1. What correlation do you see between Psalm 103 and this week's study?

2. What portions of this psalm stand out to you most?

3. Close by praying this prayer aloud:

Father,

Bless the Lord, O my soul. Let all that is within me bless His holy name! God, You are the one who forgives all my iniquity. You are the one who heals all my diseases. You are the one who redeems my life from the pit. You are the one who crowns me with steadfast love and mercy. You are the one who satisfies me with good.

And as for me? I forget, doubt, and wander. I've made self-imposed, legalistic rule-following my source, when You are my true source. I've made self-righteous knowledge about You my supply, when You are my true supply. And I've made a self-achieved facade of perfection my goal, when You are my true goal. Forgive me, Lord. I repent of my sins. Thank You for removing my transgressions from me—as far as the east is from the west!

Will You encourage and strengthen my heart? Will You fix my mind on things that are eternal? Will You keep me from being deceived? If I subtract or add anything at all to Your perfect gospel, will You convict me immediately?

You do the doing, *and I surrender my life to You, Lord—every moment of my day, each decision I make, I yield my will and way to Your perfect will and way.*

I love You too. Amen.

DAY 7

Rest, Catch Up, or Dig Deeper

WEEKLY CHALLENGE

On Days 1 and 2, you learned about the Colossians' partnership with Laodicea, union with Christ, and how unity among believers is only possible through Christ. Keeping all this in mind, write a note of encouragement to a believer or staff member of another church in your town. Thank God for how He's using them, and celebrate that you're on the same team because of Jesus's finished work. Take time to think about what might truly encourage them—don't rush it; be thoughtful.

WEEK 9

Colossians 3

Scripture to Memorize

And he is the head of the body, the church. He is the beginning, the firstborn from the dead, that in everything he might be preeminent.

Colossians 1:18

DAILY BIBLE READING

Day 1: Colossians 3:1–4

Day 2: Colossians 3:5–11

Day 3: Colossians 3:12–15

Day 4: Colossians 3:16–17

Day 5: Colossians 3:18–25

Day 6: Psalm 110

Day 7: Catch-Up Day

Corresponds to Day 349 of *The Bible Recap*.

WEEKLY CHALLENGE

See page 190 for more information.

DAY 1

Colossians 3:1–4

READ COLOSSIANS 3:1–4

Review 3:1–2.

As you learned in the introduction to Colossians (on page 111), the first half of this letter has a more doctrinal quality to it, and the second half is more practical. That practical section begins here in 3:1 with the word *if*. Essentially, *"If all I, Paul, just said is true, here's how to apply it and live in the fullness of it."*

Paul established the idea of being "raised with Christ" earlier in this letter (2:12). He was basically telling the Colossians: *"Jesus didn't stay in the tomb, so neither should we."* Your citizenship is in heaven, where Christ is. Live like it!

When Paul mentioned Christ being seated at the right hand of God, he was referencing Psalm 110. But he was also addressing the heretical idea floating around their culture that questioned whether Christ was really God (1:15, 2:9).

1. Which of the following verses are also great reminders that Christ is God? Circle all that apply.

A. Matthew 1:23

B. John 1:1

C. Philippians 2:5–7

D. Hebrews 1:3

"God with us" is His name. That's what God instructed the prophet Isaiah to pen seven hundred years before Jesus was born, just so there was no confusion (Isaiah 7:14).

In 3:2, Paul wasn't necessarily saying "things that are on earth" are evil—though some are. He was saying even seemingly harmless things can be harmful if they take the place of "things that are above."

★ 2. Write down some things in your life that take the place of "things that are above." What could removing them make room for?

Review 3:3–4.

The ancient Greek word used for *hidden* is a word you might recognize: *kryptō*. It means "to be hid, to escape notice." The early church was riddled with persecution, temptation, and trials. Knowing they were "hidden with Christ in God" would have been a great comfort and help when trying to apply Paul's encouragement to not set their minds on earthly things.

3. Though this illustration pales in comparison with the wonder of being hidden with Christ in God, for the sake of understanding the concept, label the larger nesting doll "God." Label the smaller one inside of it "me with Christ in God."

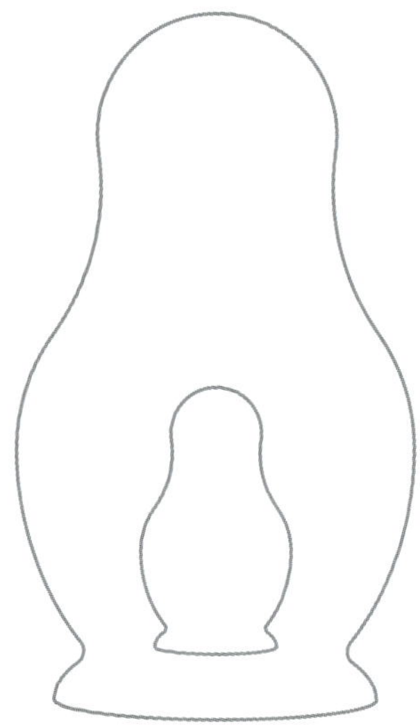

Hidden *in* Him. Not adjacent to Him, or attached to Him, or even carried on His chest in a baby sling. *Hidden—kryptō*.

Just in case the early church thought the phrase "for me to live is Christ" (Philippians 1:21) was only for special people like Paul, Paul makes it clear here: When Christ, *our* life, appears, we get to appear with Him in glory. "In glory" isn't referring to a location. It refers to a state of being—the glorified bodies described in Philippians 3:21. It's less like "in Texas" and more like "in awesomeness."

★ 4. Is this what you thought "in glory" meant? Describe.

DAY 2

Colossians 3:5–11

READ COLOSSIANS 3:5–11

Review 3:5–6.

The Greek for "put to death" here is *nekrōsate*: "to make dead." Paul told the Colossians to wipe these things out—not just suppress but eradicate. This language may seem strong at first glance.

★ 1. Have you ever meant to just dabble in your "favorite sin"—but once you dipped your toe in, you found your appetite had grown, and you'd fallen back into the old habit? Describe.

Covetousness, or the Greek *pleonexia*, refers to a greedy desire to have more. When Paul said this list is essentially idolatry, he was connecting a right attitude toward material things with worship of the one true God. Either you'll worship your flesh and things that support the satisfaction of your flesh, or you'll worship the one true God.

2. Below, put to death (by crossing out with an X) all the things you want to starve out—*nekrōsate*. Circle all the things you want to feed.

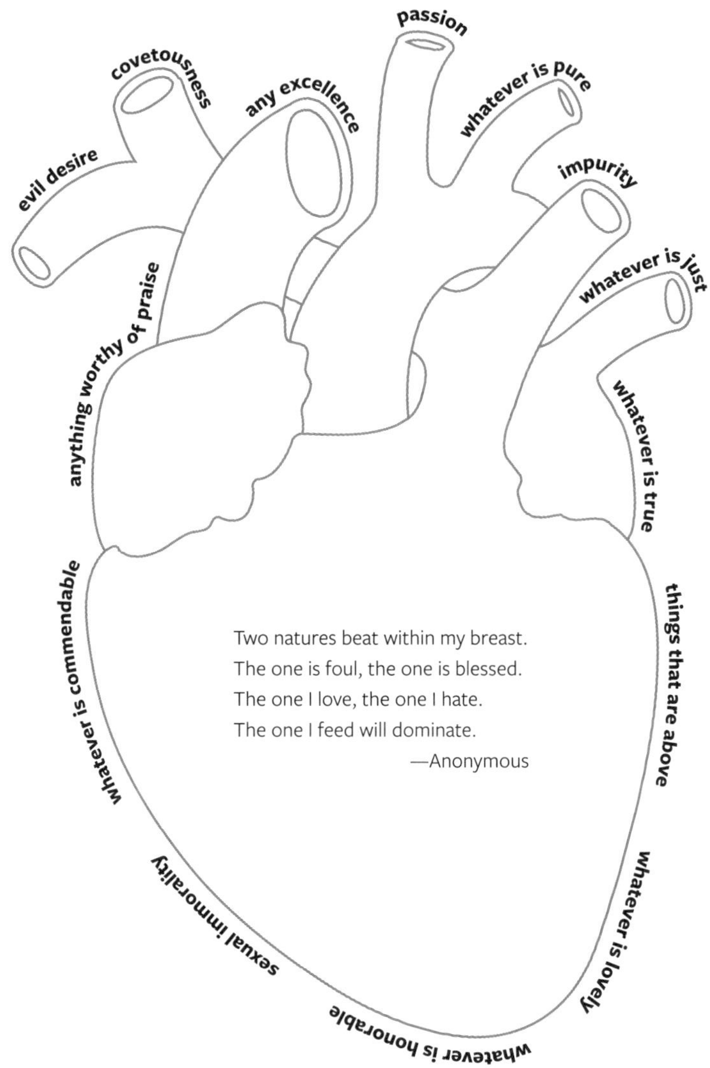

Romans 6:23 says the wages of sin is death. But don't forget the second part of that verse: "but the free gift of God is eternal life through Jesus Christ our Lord." Everything about God's design points to His heart for His people. God hates sin because it destroys His creation—it keeps them from the things that bring life instead of death.

Review 3:7–10.

Paul didn't say once you become a Christian, you'll never sin. He was using the Greek *peripateō*, which refers to how one habitually walks and conducts their life.

Are there things you dismiss as "little sins," like angrily slandering someone and thinking, *Everybody vents*, or talking obscenely, or even singing song lyrics that are ungodly while dismissing it with, *Everybody talks like this*?

★ 3. Which sins did 3:8 convict your heart of? Write some specific examples of how you could put away these things—like old clothes that don't fit you anymore.

We won't reach perfection on this side of eternity. But as Christians, we get to grow in sanctification—filled more with the knowledge of God, conformed more to the image of His Son.

It's worth noting *barbarian* didn't have a negative connotation at the time and meant something more like "foreigner." But the point remains that Paul was making a list of statuses the Colossian culture placed on people to judge their worth. And while the pursuit of Christ isn't about changing our *roles* on earth, watch how stepping into our *identity* in Christ inherently makes it impossible to keep treating one another as less. Look what the gospel does—radically changing us, from the inside out, like a heart that pumps the blood through every part, exchanging the old for the new.

DAY 3

Colossians 3:12–15

READ COLOSSIANS 3:12–15

Review 3:12–13.

In yesterday's study, Paul told the Colossians to "put off" earthly things.

1. What did Paul tell the Colossians to "put on"? Write each one on an article of clothing. On the pile of old, discarded clothes, write what Paul said to *nekrōsate* (3:5, 8).

When Paul told the Colossians to put these on "as God's chosen ones," he was pointing out that, positionally, believers are *already* God's chosen ones. Yet the "putting on" of the new self is a daily choice, like picking out an outfit each morning. As a believer, your identity is in Christ. *It's who you are.* At the same time, what you walk in each day—what you set your mind on (3:2)—is a choice. Paul said Christ is all (3:11), so choose your outfit with representing Him in mind.

The Greek for "bearing with" is *anechō*, which means "to suffer with, endure with, sustain." Acts 2:42–47 depicts the early church as having "all things in common." It wasn't a "leave your problems at the door" kind of group. The church God led His early apostles to build was communal in every way. They suffered together voluntarily. They sold their own property when someone else had a financial need.

★ 2. Does this match your church experience? Does this challenge your view of what a local church "should" be? Describe.

When Paul told the Colossians to forgive one another "as the Lord has forgiven you," he was referring to the incredible smallness of the debts others have toward us when they're compared with the biggest debt of all, which God already paid on our behalf (Matthew 18:21–35).

Review 3:14–15.

3. On the outfit below, label the cloak "love." Label the rest of the items to match the way you labeled them on page 178.

Similar to what Paul told the Corinthian church, without love, we're nothing (1 Corinthians 13:1–3). All the effort to put away the old self and put on the new will be nothing but noise to those around us if it's not done with love. Love must be the covering over it all. Don't get dressed without your cloak!

Rule here in Greek is *brabeuō*, which means "decide, arbitrate, be an umpire." Paul was telling the Colossians to let the peace of Christ be the umpire, king, and ultimate decider over their hearts—because, in Christ, believers are one body. If the right and left foot are going in opposite directions, that's not a good sign. So let the various parts of the body be at peace with one another.

Hopefully you haven't grown weary of Paul telling the Colossians to "be thankful"—because he's not done with that refrain. And remember, he wrote this letter from prison. Coming from him, that's no cheap command.

★ 4. Describe a circumstance you're facing where an earthly mindset makes thankfulness hard to imagine, but a mind "set on things above" makes way for thankfulness.

DAY 4

Colossians 3:16–17

READ COLOSSIANS 3:16–17

Today is a day of giving thanks! Yesterday, Paul ended with a command to "be thankful." And just in case you didn't catch it, he said it two more times in today's study.

In 1 Thessalonians 5:18, God says it's His will that believers "be thankful and continually give thanks to God" (AMP). This is one of three times when Scripture directly says, "This is my will for you" (see 1 Thessalonians 4:3; 1 Peter 2:15). Being thankful impacts our hearts in important ways.

Review 3:16.

★ 1. What images pop into your mind when you think of the word *dwell*?

God has always said—and will always keep saying—that He wants to dwell with His people (Exodus 25:8; Revelation 21:3).

The word used for *richly* also means "abundantly." If you put a plant in the sun only once a week, it won't thrive. And Paul was essentially telling the Colossians the same: *"Don't rent out a room to Christ once a week. Let Him dwell abundantly."* And let others who are in the body of Christ speak the Word into your life. Live in such a way that what happens at your church service spills out into the rest of your week.

It may seem like Paul was being verbose when he used three different words for songs, but these words each have unique meanings.

2. **Look up these three Greek words: *psalmos, hymnos, pneumatikos.*** Write what distinguishes them.

psalmos

hymnos

pneumatikos

If 3:16 feels unrealistic, remember that Paul's history was dark (Acts 9:4) and he experienced severe trials (2 Corinthians 11:23–28). But he was a man transformed, a man who sang while imprisoned for doing good (Acts 16:25–26). Even if you're not into singing, you're not off the hook here! Let God's praise fill your mouth (Psalm 71:8). He loves to be praised with song—even by those whose voices aren't winning any reality show contests.

3. Ask God to transform any hard places in your heart that He may dwell abundantly.

Review 3:17.

★ 4. Below, dare to write some "whatever you do's" that you haven't been thankful for before.

"And whatever I do, __________ or __________ or __________ or __________,
I'll do it in the name of the Lord."

Which ones were the hardest to write?

Because of Jesus, this life ends well for you, no matter what. Let that stir a defiant hope and thankfulness in you, no matter the circumstance.

DAY 5

Colossians 3:18–25

READ COLOSSIANS 3:18–25

Note that Paul didn't start a new letter here; he was building on all he'd already taught the Colossians. He was saying because we're called to give thanks, and sing songs, and have the mind of Christ, this should impact the way we live at home too.

And Paul wrote this *in light of* the Greco-Roman household codes that the Colossians were living under. These codes gave the father and husband of the household (*paterfamilias*) legal authority (*patria potestas*) over all those in his household.[1] Theirs was a culture where ownership of the household by the father (*pater*) was literally embedded into the word itself. Keep that in mind as you read.

Despite misconceptions, this passage brought liberation to the lowly and humility to the authoritative. Any occasion where this passage has been used to excuse mistreatment or to lord authority over one another is a misreading of the text and its original context.

Review 3:18–19.

"Submit" was not a new command in this verse—it was already expected of wives at this time in this culture. Paul merely told them how to submit *in a godly way*. The form of the verb here (*hypotassesthe*) means that Paul was telling the wives to submit voluntarily and gladly unto the Lord. It's also important to note that this passage addresses women submitting to their own husbands—*not* all women unto all men.

After Paul addressed the wives, he told the husbands to love their wives not only with a romantic love, but with a self-denying love. The Greek term is *agape*, which describes a deliberate care that prioritizes the well-being of the one being loved despite their shortcomings. It's the same type of love God has toward us. Paul didn't just tell the husbands to be nicer to their wives; he said to practice self-denial for the sake of their wives. This was *radical* in the Colossians' culture!

★ 1. Is this different from what you thought or how you've been taught? Describe.

2. Write a prayer over this issue, wherever this lesson may find you. Whether it's a place of hurt, confusion, or comfort—or even a lingering question—bring it to Him.

Review 3:20–22.

Paul addressed children directly here, which was also radical at the time—to consider them important enough to be addressed. Paul said they had a responsibility to obey their parents—but fathers had a responsibility not to be demeaning, unreasonably harsh, angry, or unforgiving. This was a vast improvement from the Greco-Roman household codes in which the father was not required to add to his authority either responsibility or care.

Review 3:23–25.

Paul gave this invitation to freedom to employees and servants: Make "eye contact" with God. Don't work well only when people are watching, so they will approve of you. *You make "eye contact" with the King of the universe when you do your work.*

There was no guaranteed fairness and there were no compliance standards for employers at this time—and Paul assured both the employer and employee, both the master and servant, of this: *Vengeance is the Lord's* (Romans 12:19). There will be no special treatment when the Lord comes to right all wrongs and reward the faithful.

★ 3. Look back to what we studied in Philippians 2:7. What form did Jesus take? How could this reality encourage you today?

He has the ultimate servant's heart. He's where the perfect *agape* is. And He's where the joy is!

4. What stood out to you most in this week's study? Why?

5. What did you learn or relearn about God and His character this week?

DAY 6

Corresponding Psalm & Prayer

READ PSALM 110

1. What correlation do you see between Psalm 110 and this week's study?

2. What portions of this psalm stand out to you most?

3. Close by praying this prayer aloud:

Father,

You're on Your throne over all the universe, yet You number the hairs on my head. Jesus, You're seated at the right hand of the Father, robed in holy garments, yet You put on flesh and came down to earth to save me. Spirit, You move in unfathomable ways, yet You speak to me in a whisper.

God, You've forgiven me, but I haven't forgiven others. You've been patient with me, but I haven't been patient with others. I've dismissed "little" sins—from the songs I sing, to the images I watch, to the words I read—and said, "Everyone does it." I've labeled big sins as little sins and insisted, "It's not a big deal." But because of Your Son, I've been raised to a better life—a new life—and I turn from those sins, big and small, and I turn to You.

Help me move from merely having good doctrine to living fully and righteously. Help me set my mind on things above. Help me walk in kindness, humility, meekness, and patience. Jesus, may Your peace rule in my heart. May Your message dwell richly in me. And may I be thankful always.

Every minute, every action, every thought, every word, may what I do be done in love. I surrender my life to You, Lord—every moment of my day, each decision I make, I yield my will and way to Your perfect will and way.

I love You too. Amen.

DAY 7

Rest, Catch Up, or Dig Deeper

WEEKLY CHALLENGE

Earlier in this study, we practiced not complaining. This week's chapter talks about what kinds of negative talk to "put away," and it tells us what kind of positive talk to "put on." This week, continue to practice not complaining, but also "put on" thanksgiving. Every day this week, end your day by writing down five new things that you're thankful for. Then, don't just be thankful—be thankful *unto the Lord*. Pray a prayer of thanks to God for those things!

WEEK 10

Colossians 4

Scripture to Memorize

For in him all the fullness
of God was pleased to
dwell, and through him
to reconcile to himself all
things, whether on earth
or in heaven, making peace
by the blood of his cross.

Colossians 1:19–20

DAILY BIBLE READING

Day 1: Colossians 4:1–4

Day 2: Colossians 4:5–6

Day 3: Colossians 4:7–9

Day 4: Colossians 4:10–13

Day 5: Colossians 4:14–18

Day 6: Psalm 107

Day 7: Catch-Up Day

Corresponds to Day 349 of *The Bible Recap.*

WEEKLY CHALLENGE

See page 211 for more information.

DAY 1

Colossians 4:1–4

READ COLOSSIANS 4:1–4

After addressing wives and husbands, children and fathers, and bondservants, Paul wrapped up his household code with a final instruction.

Review 4:1.

1. Who was Paul's final instruction for? Why do you think it's the last group he addressed in his list?

In his code, Paul certainly wasn't condoning the practice of slavery, but modern audiences may struggle with the fact that he didn't explicitly condemn it either. So here are two important notes: First, remember that Paul gave instructions for the society they *already* lived in and the structures that *already* existed. And second, stay tuned for Day 3, when we'll learn a little bit about Onesimus, one of the carriers of this letter.

But what Paul did here, without question, was point out what transcends earthly titles and allegiances altogether—they are all accountable to the same master in heaven: God.

Switching gears, Paul began his wrap-up.

Review 4:2.

2. Fill in the blanks to complete 4:2 below.

"Continue ______________ in prayer, being _______________ in it with ______________."

★ 3. What do those three words teach you about prayer?

It seems Paul pointed to a continuous cycle of future-watching—and past-reflecting—prayer: *"Lord, help us. . . . We're watching to see how You'll help us. . . . Lord, thank You for helping us."*

Review 4:3.

Paul began this letter with prayers for the Colossians (1:3), and as he concluded, he asked for their prayers. In the church, shepherds and sheep are all responsible for praying for one another. And what did he want their prayers for?

4. Circle the door below that Paul prayed God would open.

Paul prayed for more chances to do the very thing that had put him behind a locked door: "to declare the mystery of Christ."

5. What is "the mystery of Christ"? Go back to our study of 1:26–27 if you need support.

Review 4:4.

Even though he'd been proclaiming the gospel for years, Paul still sought the Colossians' prayers that he'd speak clearly when the opportunities came. His request supports a conclusion that the ability to speak the gospel clearly is a skill that's strengthened with practice and empowered through prayer.

Living your life in a way that models sanctification and points toward Jesus is a valuable ministry. But when the Lord gives us opportunity, we must be ready to *speak*. Sharing the gospel with our words can be intimidating, but like Paul, we can learn the skill that's strengthened with practice and empowered through prayer.

★ 6. To prepare to speak the gospel clearly, practice writing it clearly. What is the gospel—the good news of Jesus?

DAY 2

Colossians 4:5–6

READ COLOSSIANS 4:5–6

Having encouraged the Colossians with explanations of who they were in Christ, the power of continuous prayer, and the necessity of speaking the gospel, Paul finished his instructions by anticipating three questions: *what*, *how*, and *why*.

Review 4:5.

1. What two things did Paul encourage the Colossians to do in this verse?

A.

B.

Translated "them that are without" in the KJV, "outsiders" were nonbelievers. And certainly the Colossians would remember having just recently been outsiders themselves (1:21; 3:7). Keeping that in mind would have helped them to "walk in wisdom."

★ 2. Using what you've learned in your study of Colossians, what does walking in wisdom toward outsiders look like? Complete the table below with a few examples.

Practical Ways to Walk in Wisdom

For the first-century Colossians	For you, today

Having arrived in Rome in chains after surviving a shipwreck and a venomous snakebite (Acts 27–28), Paul understood all too well that more time isn't guaranteed to anyone. Who better, then, to encourage the Colossians to make the most of every opportunity? *"Time is fleeting,"* Paul seems to imply. *"Don't squander a single chance to bring an outsider in."*

Review 4:6.

3. How did Paul encourage the Colossians to walk in wisdom toward outsiders and make the best use of time? And why?

With gracious ____________.

So that . . .

The Greek word for *grace*—*charis*—has a few different meanings. *Charis* can point to divine favor: when God graciously gives us good things we don't deserve. *Charis* can also refer to human behavior enabled by divine grace: "that which affords joy, pleasure, delight, sweetness, charm, loveliness."[1]

This second type of *charis* is what Paul referred to here. The speech of "insiders"—those who are found in Christ—should be winsome, marked with an appropriate joy and respectful charm. Why? Because of Christ Himself.

4. Look up the passages below. What do you notice about the way Jesus spoke to outsiders?

Passage	Who was the outsider?	How did Jesus speak to the person?
John 8:1–11		
Luke 19:1–9		

★ 5. What does this teach you about the way Christians should speak to outsiders?

Paul summed up his answer to this question by saying their always-gracious speech should be "seasoned with salt." Throughout the Bible, God's people were given instructions concerning salt. Under the law, God commanded that grain offerings must be offered with salt (Leviticus 2:13). As a preservative, the salt reminded them of the covenant that God made with them and preserved.[2] In the Sermon on the Mount, Jesus told His disciples that they were "the salt of the earth" (Matthew 5:13). As a seasoning, salt enhances natural flavors and improves taste—which is a metaphor Jesus used to remind them of their influence in the world.[3]

For those "that are without," what they need the most is Jesus. Paul wanted the Colossians' speech to be so filled with grace that it seasoned the world with flavor and preserved the beauty of the gospel. Does your speech do the same?

DAY 3

Colossians 4:7–9

READ COLOSSIANS 4:7–9

Without a civil postal service—or a pony express or carrier pigeons—personal letters in the first century were delivered by trusted carriers. Today, we met the two carriers of this letter.

1. Who were the two letter carriers named in Colossians?

Review 4:7–8.

Acts 20 lists Tychicus (TIK-uh-kuhs) as one of the members of Paul's ministry team who accompanied Paul on a journey to Jerusalem with the collection that had been taken up for the persecuted church there. While Paul knew him well, the Colossians likely didn't know him at all.[1] In fact, they probably expected Epaphras—the man who planted their church—to bring them news from Paul. But Epaphras wasn't returning to Colossae just yet (more on this tomorrow). So Paul gave Tychicus a shout-out in his letter.

2. How did Paul describe Tychicus? Why did Paul send him?

★ 3. Read Ephesians 6:21–22. What do you notice?

Paul's letter carriers likely traveled from Rome to Ephesus to Colossae, delivering letters along their route.

4. On the map below, draw a few envelopes next to Rome. Then draw a line tracing their journey from Rome to Ephesus to Colossae.

Review 4:9.

★ 5. What does the text say about Onesimus, the other letter carrier?

On Day 1, you may have been left wondering why Paul didn't explicitly condemn slavery in his household code. What he *didn't* say in 4:1 may have left you troubled. So let's also look at what he didn't say here—about one of his letter carriers, Onesimus. Onesimus had a master named Philemon who lived in Colossae. (Paul wrote him a letter too.)[2] And while Onesimus was legally a runaway slave, Paul called him "our faithful and beloved brother, who is one of you." Wow!

Truly, in Christ Jesus, "there is neither slave nor free" (Galatians 3:28). Thanks be to God!

DAY 4

Colossians 4:10–13

READ COLOSSIANS 4:10–13

You made it to the *"everyone says hi"* part of Paul's letter! Today, you met four men who worked with Paul for the sake of the gospel. The first three were "men of the circumcision"—Jewish Christians.

Review 4:10–11.

★ 1. On each person below, write what these verses tell you about the men named Aristarchus, Mark, and Jesus.

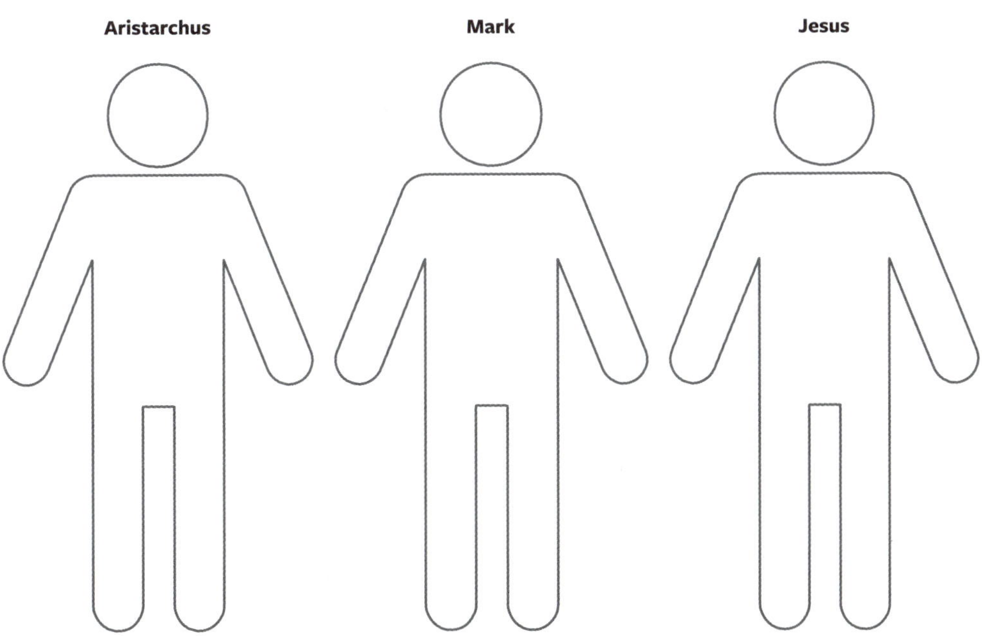

It's likely the Colossians knew much more about these men than what's written here, but today's readers might be left wondering. Thankfully, other passages in the Bible fill in some of the gaps.

2. Use the following passages to add more information to Aristarchus: Acts 19:29, Acts 20:4, and Acts 27:2.

Mark—sometimes called John Mark elsewhere in the Bible—went with Paul on his first missionary journey but left suddenly (Acts 13:13). Later, when Barnabas wanted to take his cousin John Mark on their next missionary journey, he and Paul had "a sharp disagreement" (Acts 15:39), so Barnabas and John Mark separated from Paul and Silas. Scholars have speculated as to the nature of their argument, but what's more important is what happened later.

★ 3. What did Paul tell the Colossians to do if they saw Mark again? What does that tell you? Why does it matter?

4. Use the information you just learned and the following passages to add more details to Mark: Philemon 24 and 2 Timothy 4:11.

And as for Jesus/Justus? Jesus was a common name for first-century Jewish men, but there aren't any other clues about this particular Jesus. We'll have to wait until the kingdom to find out more about him.

Review 4:12–13.

A fourth man sent his greetings, and this one was certainly well-known to the Colossians: Epaphras. As a reminder, he founded the church in Colossae and his report to Paul prompted this letter (1:7–9). According to Paul, Epaphras also worked hard for the spread of the gospel in two towns near

Colossae—Laodicea and Hierapolis. The believers in those towns likely would have been eager to see him, and he to see them.

5. Read Philemon 23 (it's a verse, not a chapter). Why didn't Epaphras return to the Colossians to deliver Paul's letter?

While he couldn't return to Colossae, Epaphras used his time to pray for his brothers and sisters, even "struggling" in those prayers. The Greek word Paul used—*agōnizomai*—suggests a physical fight with difficulties and dangers.[1] Some translations say Epaphras "labored" or "wrestled" in prayer. And what was he agonizing over? That the Colossians might "stand mature and fully assured in all the will of God." (See also 1:9–12.)

6. Do you "struggle in your prayers" on behalf of someone else? That they may "stand mature and fully assured in all the will of God"? Ask God to bring someone's name to mind, and write a prayer below on their behalf.

DAY 5

Colossians 4:14–18

READ COLOSSIANS 4:14–18

Review 4:14.

In today's reading, two others sent their well wishes: Luke and Demas. Luke went with Paul on a few journeys, including the one that led to a shipwreck and Paul's captivity in Rome. Luke is the one who wrote the gospel of Luke and the book of Acts. At this point, Demas was one of Paul's co-laborers, but later, "in love with this present world," he deserted the work (2 Timothy 4:10). May his story remind us to wrestle in prayer for our ministers that they would stand mature and steadfast in the will of God.

Review 4:15–17.

Then Paul sent some greetings of his own and gave some instructions about the letter.

1. Use 4:15–17 to complete the postcards below.

It's worth noting that there is some debate over who Nympha was. Some early translations use Nymphas—the male form of the name—and state that the church met in *his* house. Many theologians and translators agree, though, that Nympha was a woman—and one wealthy enough to own a home used for a gathering.[1] And if that's accurate, she was certainly among good company of other faithful female servants in the first-century church, joining the ranks of Lydia (Acts 16:14–15), Phoebe (Romans 16:1–2), Prisca (Romans 16:3–5), Junia (Romans 16:7), and more.

Greetings!

—Paul

To:

After you read this letter, pass it on.

—Paul

To:

Greetings!

—Paul

To:

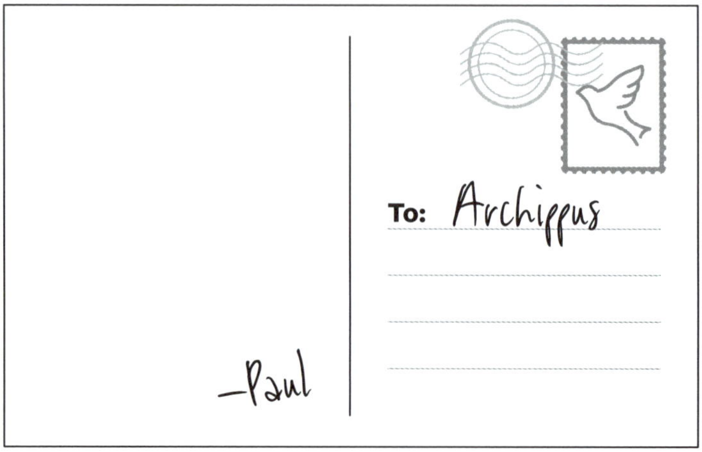

Lists of names in the Bible can seem skippable. But consider this: Over the past few days, you've read how a Jewish Pharisee, a Gentile doctor, a wealthy woman, a runaway slave, and a host of others labored together for the sake of the gospel. They prayed for one another, supported one another, bore with one another, forgave one another, and encouraged one another. These names (and the stories they tell) hold an important perspective for us—don't miss it!

Ekklēsia, the Greek word for church, means "an assembly of Christians gathered for worship in a religious meeting,"[2] not a building. *These people* were the church. And through their faithfulness and by the grace of God, you are the *ekklēsia* too!

★ 2. Whose story stood out to you this week? Why?

★ 3. If your name were in a letter to your church, what would you want written about you?

Review 4:18.

Timothy likely served as Paul's scribe for this letter, but before they sent it, Paul checked the draft and approved it[3]—literally signing off. In his own handwriting, he told the Colossians to remember his chains. Because he had acknowledged that he was both in prison and a slave to Christ, scholars are divided over whether his words were literal or metaphorical.

4. Why might Paul have wanted them to remember his chains? Complete the table below.

If Paul meant the literal chains he wore in captivity (see 4:3), then . . .	If Paul meant the metaphorical chains of a servant of God (see Colossians 1:7; Romans 1:1; Philemon 1:1), then . . .

Like he did in 4:6, Paul used the word *charis* again—*grace*. And this time, his meaning wasn't about human speech; it was all about God. In a divine sense, *charis* means "of the merciful kindness by which God, exerting his holy influence upon souls, turns them to Christ, keeps, strengthens, increases them in Christian faith, knowledge, affection, and kindles them to the exercise of the Christian virtues."[4]

God turned Paul to Himself. By His grace, He kept him, strengthened him, and increased Paul's faith, knowledge, and affection for Him. Paul prayed the same divine favor over the Colossians. He's where the grace is, and He's where the joy is!

5. What stood out to you most in this week's study? Why?

6. What did you learn or relearn about God and His character this week?

DAY 6

Corresponding Psalm & Prayer

READ PSALM 107

1. What correlation do you see between Psalm 107 and this week's study?

2. What portions of this psalm stand out to you most?

3. Close by praying this prayer aloud:

Father,

You are good, and Your steadfast love endures forever! I cried out to You, and You delivered me. I needed saving, and You saved me.

I needed forgiveness, and You forgave me. Truly, I have seen Your works, Your wonderful deeds in the deep.

But Lord, my words haven't always reflected Your goodness. At times, I've spoken too much, and my speech hasn't always been gracious. I haven't seasoned it with salt, but with fire—sarcasm, gossip, complaining, and lies. And at other times, I haven't spoken enough; instead—I've been silent about what matters most: You. *Forgive me.*

May my words be gracious, seasoning the world with flavor and preserving the beauty of the gospel. You've forgiven me, and like Jesus commanded, I want to go and sin no more! You've redeemed me, and like the psalmist wrote, I want to say so! You've saved me, and like Paul taught, I want to be ready to speak. When the time comes for me to speak the gospel, will You give me Your words and multiply my efforts?

I surrender my life to You, Lord—every moment of my day, each decision I make, I yield my will and way to Your perfect will and way.

I love You too. Amen.

DAY 7

Rest, Catch Up, or Dig Deeper

WEEKLY CHALLENGE

On Day 1, you practiced writing the gospel—the good news of Jesus. Commit your gospel presentation to memory, and practice speaking it out loud to a friend this week. Pray and watch for an opportunity to share it with someone who doesn't know Him, then graciously speak the good news of Jesus. "Let the redeemed of the Lord say so" (Psalm 107:2)!

FOR GROUP LEADERS

Thank you for using this study and leading others through it as well! Each week has a wide variety of content (daily Bible reading, content and questions, Scripture memorization, weekly challenge, and resources) to help the reader develop a range of spiritual disciplines. Feel free to include as much or as little of that in your meetings as you'd like. The details provided in How to Use This Study (pp. 7–9) will be helpful to you and all your group members, so be sure to review that information together!

It's up to you and your group how you'd like to structure your meetings, but we suggest including time for discussion of the week's study and Bible text, mutual encouragement, and prayer. You may also want to practice your Scripture memory verses together as a group or in pairs. As you share with each other, "consider how to stir up one another to love and good works" (Hebrews 10:24) and "encourage one another and build one another up" (1 Thessalonians 5:11).

Here are some sample questions to help facilitate discussion. This is structured as a weekly study, but if your group meets at a different frequency, you may wish to adjust the questions accordingly. Cover as many questions as time allows, or feel free to come up with your own. And don't forget to check out the additional resources we've linked for you at MyDGroup.org/Resources/PhilCol.

Sample Discussion Questions

What questions did this week's study or Bible text bring up for you?

What stood out to you in this week's study?

What did you notice about God and His character?

How were you challenged by your study of the Bible text? Is there anything you want to change in light of what you learned?

How does what you learned about God affect the way you live in community?

What correlation did you see between the psalm from Day 6 and this week's study of Philippians (or Colossians)?

Have you felt God working in you through the weekly challenge? If so, how?

Is your love for God's Word increasing as we go through this study? If so, how?

Did anything you learned increase your joy in knowing Jesus?

ACKNOWLEDGMENTS

Laura Buchelt, Emily Pickell, Abbey Dane, Emma Dotter, Kirsten McCloskey, and Liz Suggs—thank you for your incredible research, creativity, wisdom, humility, and laughter. It's truly a *blast* to study God's Word with you all!

Rachel Mantooth—for sharing your incredible gift of hospitality as house mom, for your persistent prayer and encouragement, and for all the ways you serve and lead D-Group beautifully!

Olivia Le—thank you for making our writing summits run seamlessly!

Lisa Jackson—you continue to be such a gift as a guide, agent, and friend.

Phil Collins.

And to the rest of the incredible D-Group Team—Rachel Mantooth, Lindsay Ruhter, Warwick Fuller, Jane Long, Meg Mitchell, Evaline Asmah, and our board, leaders, members, and church partners around the world—I love being on mission with you!

NOTES

Week 1: Day 1

1. "What Are the Responsibilities of Deacons in the Church?" Got Questions, https://www.gotquestions.org/deacons-church.html; Benjamin Merkle, "The Biblical Qualifications and Responsibilities of Deacons, 9Marks, March 31, 2010, https://www.9marks.org/article/biblical-qualifications-and-responsibilities-deacons/.

Week 1: Day 3

1. "G627—apologia—Strong's Greek Lexicon (ESV)," Blue Letter Bible, https://www.blueletterbible.org/lexicon/g627/esv/mgnt/0-1/.

Week 1: Day 5

1. "Philippians 1:15–17 Commentary," Precept Austin, November 18, 2022, https://www.preceptaustin.org/philippians_115-17.

2. Kevin Kruse, "Stephen Covey: 10 Quotes That Can Change Your Life," July 16, 2012, https://www.forbes.com/sites/kevinkruse/2012/07/16/the-7-habits/#.

Week 2: Day 2

1. "Philippians 1—Paul's Love and Concern for the Philippians," Enduring Word, https://enduringword.com/bible-commentary/philippians-1/.

2. *Heidelberg Catechism*, Lord's Day 1, https://www.heidelberg-catechism.com/pdf/lords-days/Heidelberg-Catechism.pdf.

Week 2: Day 4

1. Tremper Longman III and David E. Garland, eds., *The Expositor's Bible Commentary: Ephesians–Philemon*, vol. 12, rev. ed. (Zondervan, 2006), 208–210.

2. "G684—apōleia—Strong's Greek Lexicon (ESV)," Blue Letter Bible, https://www.blueletterbible.org/lexicon/g684/esv/mgnt/0-1/.

Week 4: Day 1

1. Bruce B. Barton, et al., *Life Application Bible Commentary: Philippians, Colossians, and Philemon* (Tyndale House Publishers, 1995), 77.

Week 4: Day 4

1. Warren W. Wiersbe, *Be Joyful: New Testament Commentary–Philippians* (David C. Cook, 2008), 115.

Week 4: Day 5

1. "Philippians 3—Leaving Law and Pressing On to Jesus," Enduring Word, https://enduringword.com/bible-commentary/philippians-3/.

Week 5: Day 2

1. Gordon D. Fee, *Philippians*, IVP New Testament Commentary Series (IVP Academic, 1999), 174–175.

Week 5: Day 3

1. Gordon D. Fee, *Philippians*, IVP New Testament Commentary Series (IVP Academic, 1999), 185.
2. Fee, *Philippians*, 185.

Week 6: Day 2

1. Bruce B. Barton et al., *Life Application Bible Commentary: Philippians, Colossians, and Philemon* (Tyndale House Publishers, 1995), 140.
2. Barton et al., *Life Application Bible Commentary*, 142.

Week 6: Day 4

1. "4678. sophia, Strong's Greek Lexicon," HELPS Word-Studies, Discovery Bible, https://biblehub.com/greek/4678.htm.
2. W. Ian Thomas, *The Saving Life of Christ* (Zondervan, 1961), 150.

Week 7: Day 1

1. N. T. Wright, *Colossians and Philemon: An Introduction and Commentary*, Tyndale New Testament Commentaries, vol. 12 (IVP Academic, 1986), 70.
2. Thomas L. Constable, "Notes on Colossians" (1:16 commentary), Sonic Light, https://soniclight.com/tcon/notes/html/colossians/colossians.htm.

Week 7: Day 4

1. Alan J. Thompson, *Colossians and Philemon: An Introduction and Commentary*, Tyndale New Testament Commentaries, vol. 12 (InterVarsity Press, 2022), 78.
2. N. T. Wright, *Colossians and Philemon: An Introduction and Commentary*, Tyndale New Testament Commentaries, vol. 12 (IVP Academic, 1986), 93.
3. Thomas L. Constable, "Notes on Colossians" (1:27 commentary), Sonic Light, https://soniclight.com/tcon/notes/html/colossians/colossians.htm.

Week 8: Day 1

1. "Colossians 2—Answering the Colossian Heresy," Enduring Word, https://enduringword.com/bible-commentary/colossians-2/.

Week 8: Day 3

1. See "What Is the Meaning of Vain Deceit in Colossians 2:8?" Got Questions, https://www.gotquestions.org/vain-deceit.html.

Week 8: Day 4

1. "What Is the Christian View of Asceticism / Monasticism?" Got Questions, https://www.gotquestions.org/Christian-asceticism-monasticism.html.

Week 9: Day 5

1. Clinton E. Arnold, *Ephesians* (Zondervan, 2010), 373.

Week 10: Day 2

1. "G5485—charis—Strong's Greek Lexicon (KJV)," Blue Letter Bible, https://www.blueletterbible.org/lexicon/g5485/kjv/tr/0-1/.

2. *ESV Women's Study Bible* (Crossway, 2020), 166n2:11–13.
3. *ESV Women's Study Bible* (Crossway, 2020), 1507n5:13.

Week 10: Day 3

1. "Colossians 4—Prayer Life, Personal Witness, and Final Greetings," Enduring Word, https://enduringword.com/bible-commentary/colossians-4/.
2. *ESV Women's Study Bible* (Crossway, 2020), 2305.

Week 10: Day 4

1. "G75—agōnizomai—Strong's Greek Lexicon (ESV)," Blue Letter Bible, https://www.blueletterbible.org/lexicon/g75/mgnt/mgnt/0-1/.

Week 10: Day 5

1. Tremper Longman III and David E. Garland, eds., *The Expositor's Bible Commentary: Ephesians–Philemon*, vol. 12, rev. ed. (Zondervan, 2006), 355–357.
2. "G1577–ekklēsia—Strong's Greek Lexicon (KJV)," Blue Letter Bible, https://www.blueletterbible.org/lexicon/g1577/kjv/tr/0-1/.
3. Longman III and Garland, *Expositor's Bible Commentary*, 359–360.
4. "G5485—charis—Strong's Greek Lexicon (kjv)," Blue Letter Bible, https://www.blueletterbible.org/lexicon/g5485/kjv/tr/0-1/.

ABOUT THE EDITOR

TARA-LEIGH COBBLE'S zeal for biblical literacy is at the heart of everything she creates. Her goal is to help people read, understand, and love the Bible. Her daily podcast, *The Bible Recap*, guides listeners through a chronological one-year reading plan. The podcast has over 500 million downloads and reached number one on the Apple Podcast charts in All Categories. She created and leads D-Group International, which has grown into an international network of nearly 400 weekly Bible studies that meet in homes, in churches, and online. A *Wall Street Journal* bestselling author, she also writes and hosts a daily radio feature called *The God Shot*, and leads trips to Israel to study the Bible on-site. Tara-Leigh lives in Dallas, Texas, where she has no pets, children, or anything else that might die if she forgets to feed it.

For more information: TaraLeighCobble.com | TheBibleRecap.com | MyDGroup.org | Israelux.com
Social media: @taraleighcobble | @thebiblerecap | @mydgroup | @israeluxtours

MINISTRIES

THE BIBLE RECAP—*READ THE BIBLE*

Est. 2019 | TheBibleRecap.com
Have you ever closed your Bible and thought, *What did I just read?* In about eight minutes a day, our summary walks you through the one-year chronological plan. Available in podcast, YouTube, and book form. Other supplemental resources available for adults and children.

D-GROUP INTERNATIONAL—*STUDY THE BIBLE*

Est. 2009 | MyDGroup.org
Men's and women's Bible study groups that meet weekly—in homes, online, and in churches around the world. D-Groups work through a series of 40 studies that cover the entire Bible over the course of a decade.

ISRAELUX—*EXPERIENCE THE BIBLE*

Est. 2014 | Israelux.com
Offering a deluxe tour, incredible dining experiences, luxury accommodations, and life-changing teaching at biblical sites. The beauty of Israel is also captured in TLC's book *Israel: Beauty, Light, and Luxury*, a *Wall Street Journal* bestseller.